WHAT'S NEXT FOR ME?

The Need for Clarity

Praise for What's Next for Me

"Jamie's career is a masterclass in the pivot—moving strongly into new arenas, absorbing what matters, and translating lived experience into practical wisdom. I've seen him apply these perspectives to himself for years, making deliberate shifts in real time in both his work and his life. He offers excellent perspective, and his book distills the signals, shifts, and technological realities of our era into guidance that pushes professionals to make braver, higher-quality decisions about what comes next. The result is a way of thinking built to help readers move toward the life they're actually meant to lead."

— **Matt Doan**, Founder, Corporate Graduation

"Jamie has lived through all the tech revolutions of the past three decades, and he's got the scars and wisdom to prove it. Covering ground from the early days of the Internet, when Yahoo! was king and you had to print your driving directions from MapQuest, to the rise of AI's still-ongoing disruption, this book is both a front-row seat to digital transformation and a survival guide for anyone trying to build a meaningful career in today's anything-goes tech and business environments.

What makes Jamie's story compelling isn't just the prestigious firms or billion-dollar deals: it's his relentless curiosity about how technology impacts real people, and his honest reckoning with burnout, corporate politics, and the courage it takes to redefine success on your own terms. Most consultants will sell you slides about digital transformation (I often had Jamie up until 3am working on those slides making sure all the fonts matched). But he also lived the messy reality behind them, including stress so intense that he had hives—which a doctor in a questionable Dallas neighborhood first suspected to be more, er, social.

If you're questioning your corporate path or trying to make sense of the AI wave while everyone's pretending to be an expert, you'll appreciate Jamie's refusal to bullshit you about what actually works."

— **Peter Maloof**, Innovator and, admittedly, Digital Transformation Specialist

Working with Jamie was a gamechanger for me. We worked together by chance and under his mentorship, I was able to turn my career on its side and forge a new path for myself. His expertise, leadership, outlook, and mindset are invaluable, and his friendship and support are a treasure. No exaggeration, Jamie is someone who has truly changed my life.

— **Jenn Carlson**, Digital Transformation Consultant

What's Next for Me? The Need for Clarity
Published by Digital Dirty Work

ISBN (Paperback): 979-8-9936420-0-0
ISBN (eBook): 979-8-9936420-1-7
© 2025 Jamie Hammond

Printed in the United States of America

First Edition 2025
1 2 3 4 5 6 7 8 9 10
12/01/25

To those reflecting and reinventing themselves
in real time, this is for you.

Contents

Foreword

BY MUKUL PANDYA

When Jamie Hammond walked into my office at the Wharton School of the University of Pennsylvania in 2001, the digital revolution was in its infancy. Google had maybe 1,000 employees. Amazon was still mostly books. And *Knowledge@Wharton*—the digital thought leadership platform that my colleagues and I had launched just two years earlier—was fighting to grow in a world that didn't yet understand why business insights shouldn't wait for quarterly print runs.

Jamie came aboard to help us figure out how to raise the funds to sustain this experiment, which eventually grew into a portfolio of publications in multiple languages with more than 3 million users, in addition to a high-school version and a radio show. His title said sales and marketing, but what he really brought was something far more valuable: a bone-deep understanding that technology only matters when it serves human needs. Twenty-plus years later, as I read his remarkable memoir, I realize he's been carrying that same truth through every technological revolution since.

"What's Next for Me?" is not a run-of-the-mill business book. It's a survival guide written by someone who's been buried alive by corporate transformations and lived to tell the tale—again and again. More importantly, it's a permission slip for anyone who's ever sat in a windowless conference room at 2 AM, tweaking PowerPoint slides, wondering if this is really what success looks like.

I spent more than two decades at Wharton, curating and publishing insights from the world's leading thinkers. I've interviewed superstar faculty as well as CEOs who've built empires. I have watched companies succumb to disruption they didn't see coming. But Jamie's story is different. Why? Because he is not theorizing from some ivory tower. He has been in the trenches when Y2K was going to end civilization, when the dot-com bubble burst, when eCommerce was going to kill retail, and now when AI threatens to make us all obsolete. Each time, he adapted, learned, and most importantly—stayed human.

The book you're holding is essentially three stories woven into one. First, it's a front-row seat to the digital transformation of American business, from MapQuest printouts to ChatGPT prompts. Jamie was there when a major Maintenance, Repair, and Operations (MRO) company figured out B2B eCommerce; when a huge Chicago-based quick-serve restaurant (QSR) built a loyalty app that now drives 40% of their revenues; when prestigious consulting firms started eating their young in the name of "Areas for Development." These are war stories, complete with the scars to prove their authenticity.

Second, it's a brutally honest examination of what corporate success actually costs. The stress-induced hives in a Dallas hotel. The divorce that comes from choosing employer expectations over family presence. The soul-crushing realization that even at a Big Three firm—the supposed pinnacle of consulting—you're just making slides that someone will critique based on their mood that day. Jamie doesn't sugarcoat the price of admission to the corporate elite, and that honesty is both refreshing and necessary.

But the third story—the one that makes this book essential reading—is about reclaiming agency in a world designed to strip it away. It's about recognizing that the same company that calls you "talent" will "transition" you out without blinking. It's about understanding that burnout isn't a badge of honor but a warning sign. It's about the radical act of investing in yourself through coaching, creating space for what matters, and building something that can't be taken away by the next restructuring.

What strikes me most is Jamie's pattern recognition. He has identified the recurring cycles that every technology follows: Experimentation, Standardization, Commoditization. He has mapped the cast of characters that appear in every transformation: the Visionary CEO, the Skeptical CFO, the Fast Follower. Most importantly, he has recognized that while technologies change at exponential rates, human nature remains remarkably constant.

This school-of-hard-knocks wisdom is exactly what is missing from most discussions about AI today. While everyone is panicking about ChatGPT replacing jobs, Jamie is asking the questions that truly matter: Who is threatened by this? What problem are we actually solving? Are we moving at technology velocity, organizational velocity, or market velocity? These are not exactly academic frameworks; they are battle-tested scenarios drawn from watching million-dollar implementations succeed and fail.

Jamie's "Persona-First Transformation" approach, refined during the large MRO company implementation, feels especially relevant now. Before we rush to implement AI everywhere, we should ask: Who specifically will use this? What problem does it solve for them? It's the same discipline that turned "Mike the Maintenance Manager" from a PowerPoint slide into a north star for one of the most successful B2B digital transformations ever.

But perhaps the book's greatest gift is permission. Permission to say "my family comes first" to a boss. Permission to walk away from soul-sucking work without another job lined up. Permission to value your strengths over your "Areas for Development." Permission to believe that your experience—even if it predates TikTok—has value in navigating what the future holds.

For those of us who remember dial-up internet, who have survived multiple "transformations" and "reorganizations", who have been told we are dinosaurs for questioning the latest big bang approach—Jamie's book is vindication. Our scar tissue is a strategic advantage. Our pattern recognition is priceless. Our ability to translate between technological eras is exactly what organizations need, whether they know it or not.

As I write this, AI dominates every business conversation. The same breathless promises, the same vendor hype, the same anxiety I've watched cycle through for decades. But here's what I know: The winners won't be those with the best technology. They'll be those who understand that transformation is human work first, technical work second. They'll be those who have failed enough to recognize the warning signs. They'll be those who can bridge between what was, what is, and what will be.

Jamie Hammond is one of those bridges. And if you're reading this, you probably are too. You just might not know it yet.

Mukul Pandya is an Associate Fellow at Oxford University's Saïd Business School.

He is the founding former editor-in-chief and executive director of Knowledge@Wharton (K@W), the web-based journal of research and business analysis published by the Wharton School of the University of Pennsylvania. He edited and managed K@W for more than 22 years until his retirement in 2020. In 2020-21, he was a Senior Fellow at the research centres Wharton AI for Business and Wharton Customer Analytics. Mukul has won four awards for investigative journalism and has more than 40 years of experience as a writer and editor. His articles have appeared in The Wall Street Journal, The New York Times, The Economist, Time magazine, The Philadelphia Inquirer and other publications.

He co-authored Lasting Leadership, Knowledge@Wharton on building corporate value and has written, co-authored or edited four other books. In 2025, he co-authored Creativity in the Age of AI: Toolkits for the Modern Mind with Jerry Wind and Deborah Yao.

What's Next For You? (And Why That Question Matters Right Now)

Let's be honest: you picked up this book because something feels... off.

Maybe you've been doing your job well for a decade or more, and suddenly the ground shifted under your feet. AI entered the conversation, and now every meeting starts with some version of: "How does this change everything?" Maybe you're watching competitors move faster, your skills feel less certain, and you're wondering if you've been building toward something that's about to become obsolete. Or maybe—and this one stings—you're realizing that everything you've optimized for (the promotions, the prestige, the title) isn't actually making you happy.

If any of this resonates with you, you're not alone. And more importantly, you're asking exactly the right question at exactly the right time.

Why "What's Next For Me?" Is The Question Of This Moment

We're in the middle of something massive. Not the beginning: we're past the hype cycle and into the real reckoning. Generative AI isn't coming anymore; it's just *here*. And unlike the internet, which gave us a decade to figure it out, or mobile, which gave us five years, AI is moving at warp speed. The businesses, roles, and skill sets that matter today might look completely different in three years. Look at the recent headlines: layoffs at Amazon, Microsoft, Accenture, and more, all attributed to AI "gains."

But what nobody's telling you is that you're actually better prepared for this than you think.

If you've been working in any technical or business capacity over the last 25 years, you've already survived multiple revolutions. You've seen technologies that were supposed to change everything either transform industries or disappear quietly. You've probably worked through a dot-com crash, a financial crisis, a pandemic that forced your entire operation remote, or all three. Your muscle memory for adaptation is stronger than you realize.

The problem is, you might not recognize it as such.

Most career advice right now breaks into two camps. One says: "Learn AI or get left behind"—which is true, but incomplete and anxiety-inducing. The other says: "Your soft skills are timeless"— which is also true, but also insufficient when your industry is being restructured around you. What's missing is the lived experience of someone who's actually navigated multiple technological upheavals, made real mistakes (and learned from them), and figured out how to stay relevant without losing themselves in the process.

That's what this book is.

What You'll Find Here (And What You Won't)

This isn't a guide to prompt engineering or a technical manual on implementing AI systems. You can get that anywhere. What you'll get here instead is something rarer and, I'd argue, more valuable: a map of how to think about massive change, drawn by someone who's lived through it multiple times.

I've built a career watching technologies transform industries—and watching organizations, teams, and people either rise to meet that change or get crushed by it. I've watched the internet go from "what is that?" to the foundation of nearly everything. I've helped companies figure out how to sell products online when that was revolutionary. I've designed loyalty programs that now drive billions in revenue. I've also been laid off from a prestigious consulting firm when I no longer fit their mold, and I've rebuilt from that rubble in ways that surprised me.

Along the way, I've seen patterns. Patterns in how change happens. Patterns in how organizations fail at transformation. Patterns in how people either thrive through disruption or burn out. Patterns that repeat, with striking consistency, regardless of whether the technology is eCommerce or AI.

This book walks you through those patterns, and more importantly, shows you how to use them.

The Questions We'll Explore Together

Throughout these chapters, we'll tackle the things that actually keep professionals awake at night:

- **How do you build a meaningful career** when the ground keeps moving under your feet?
- **What does success actually look like** when you stop letting employers define it?
- **How do you stay relevant** through multiple technology waves without becoming a commoditized expert?
- **What patterns repeat** across different revolutions, and how can you exploit them to your advantage?
- **When does ambition become self-destructive,** and how do you recognize burnout before your body forces you to?
- **Can you maintain boundaries** in demanding environments

and still advance—or is that a fantasy?

- **Who are you outside your job title?** And what happens when you actually have to answer that question?
- **What do you do** when your values no longer align with your employer's?
- **How do you recover** from rejection, layoffs, and the ego blow of being "transitioned out"?
- **Can you start from scratch** as an independent consultant, and should you?
- **How do you leverage** all your hard-won experience without getting trapped by it?

This isn't theoretical: I've lived all of the above. Some I've handled well, and others I've fumbled badly. All of them have taught me something that I think you need to know, or can at least learn from.

What I'm Trying to Give You

Here's my intention with this book: I want to give you permission.

Permission to stop pretending that the old playbook—show up, work hard, climb the ladder, let the company define success—is still the only way. Permission to recognize that you're probably further along on your own journey than you realize. Permission to question whether that "perfect opportunity" is actually perfect, or just perfectly packaged. Permission to walk away from something prestigious if it's costing you your peace. Permission to invest in yourself before someone else gives you permission.

But more than that, I want to give you a toolkit. I can't give you a formula, because there isn't one, and every situation is different. Your next chapter will look different from mine. But I want you to see a set of patterns, and I want you to have a way of thinking about change.

I want you to know these real stories from the trenches—complete with mistakes, victories, pivots, and the moments when I finally understood something crucial.

You're going to read about:

- **How I stumbled through the early digital era** and what I learned about building value in industries that didn't exist yet
- **How I climbed into prestigious firms** and why the climb felt emptier than I expected
- **How I got burned out and didn't see it coming** until my body literally broke out in hives
- **How I got pushed out of a major consulting firm** and why it turned out to be the best thing that happened to me
- **How I rebuilt from scratch** as an independent consultant without a safety net
- **How I'm navigating AI right now**, at 50, with the same patterns I've seen before but moving three times faster

Each chapter is going to end with real, distilled takeaways—not because I think I have all the answers, but because you deserve actionable wisdom, not just stories.

The Real Work

Reading this book won't change your life; I can't do that for you. What I can do, though, is show you what's possible: I can show you that other people have walked through the fire of technological disruption, corporate rejection, and identity crisis—and come out the other side not just intact, but actually more themselves.

The real work starts after you close this book. It starts with the hard questions you ask yourself; with the conversations you have with people you trust; with the boundaries you set; with the risks you take; and with the version of success you define for yourself, not the one society handed you.

My job is just to hand you a map. Your job is to walk the path.

Why Now Matters

AI isn't coming in five years. It's here now. And the professionals who'll thrive in the next five years won't be the ones who panic or the ones who pretend everything will stay the same. They'll be the ones who recognize what's happening, learn from how similar shifts have played out before, and position themselves with clear ideas instead of fear.

You've already survived multiple revolutions. You know more than you think about how to adapt. You've built skills that transfer across technologies—the ability to sell a company's product or yourself, to lead, to understand what customers actually need, and to know the difference between hype and reality.

What you need now is perspective. You need to see your own journey clearly, without the noise. You need to know that the questions you're asking, like "What's next for me?", "Who am I outside this job?", and "What do I actually want?" really mean something.

These are the right questions.

This book is your answer to that.

So let's start here: you've navigated change before. You've built things. You've learned from failure. You're asking the hard questions.

You're more ready than you think.

Let's figure out what's actually next.

Note: Each chapter will end with clear takeaways—insights earned through real experience, not theory. Use them. Question them. Adapt them to your own situation. And most importantly, remember: your journey doesn't have to look like mine. It just has to be true to you.

CHAPTER 1

What The Fuck Is The Internet? Or: The Confusion You Feel About AI Now Is Exactly What People Felt About The Internet In 1995

You Can't Predict Which Technology Will Matter, But You Can Recognize When People Stop Questioning It

It was the beginning of a new age—or at least that's how I like to think about it. You've heard it before: dial up speeds leading to slow loading pages, basic websites, and forget social media, in the early days it was all about IM'ing (Instant Messaging) and chat rooms. Computer labs started becoming big things, large servers were being bought at a rapid pace, AOL was mailing out discs just so you could install its software on your computers to go online. It was a very exciting time, and no one had any idea what it would lead to.

My first teacher to embrace this was at the University of Dayton. He started us off really easy, taking us through this vast digital (and I use that word lightly) landscape to show us some of the cooler bells and whistles. I remember coming home from his class one day to my close friend, Noel, sitting on the couch of the house we lived in. When I tried to explain what I just learned, I could see the confusion on his face. Not one for ever holding back, he almost yelled his question: "What the fuck is the internet!?" If I could have just captured that moment on film or had an audio recording of it, I would play it continuously. Alas, no iPhones around back then.

I think about that moment a lot now, especially when I see the same confusion on people's faces when they first encounter ChatGPT or hear about large language models. It's the same kind of bewilderment; it's still that same mix of skepticism and curiosity. Just recently I had a manager ask me, "But what does it actually *do*?" The tools change, but the basic human reaction to transformative tech feels like a constant. And just like with the internet, the ones who lean into the weirdness instead of running from it are the ones who'll end up ahead.

The really genius thing my professor at Dayton did was that he had a light bulb moment where he seemed to tell himself, "This thing is out there in the ether: why do we need to be here in class to talk about it and do show and tell? I can literally have them go do some cyber sleuthing, find some clues/answers, and message me by email!"

Brilliant. This man was thinking about something so groundbreaking for academia at the time, with the great benefit of taking down the amount of hours he had to spend on campus or in class, that I am shocked he wasn't either: A) kicked out of school for what I would have imagined was frowned upon in stuffy old academia, or B) had a line of professors out his door trying to see if they could replicate his success in decreasing the 9-5 aspect of the job they were all signed up for.

I don't want to make it seem like we did not have class at all—we did—but it did decrease the face-to-face aspect of it slightly. I think of this now and can't help but tie it back to our current state and how people suffered during the "work from home" part of the Covid pandemic. I'd like to think I've been incorporating this working style since 1995. Don't get me wrong—I definitely see many benefits of the face-to-face aspect in life, but clearly there are some advantages to working remotely.

Lessons went from pretty easy (he'd tell us to "log on" to Yahoo maps or MapQuest and map out a route to somewhere), to somewhat challenging: go learn HTML and try to create your own web page. There were things like deadlines, and he would be helpful if we hit a stumbling block, but in terms of getting us really comfortable and more knowledgeable on what was out there, he did a fantastic job.

In fact, I need to find this person and send him a note thanking him for steering me in a direction and into an industry that would impact and influence the rest of my career. I also need to pay it forward and do my best to educate those out there on the latest and greatest with the current situation now, so some day a student somewhere can run back to tell their friends about what new and fascinating things they just learned and get the same cursing response I got from my old friend. It obviously stuck with me, and is exactly what we are seeing now with the advent of AI and ChatGPT.

First Jobs In The Digital Sphere After College

Confidence + Minimal Real Knowledge = The Recipe For Growth

So here I am, freshly minted graduate out of the University of Dayton, about to embark on life after college. I'm full of piss and vinegar, as the saying goes, and ready to take on the world. Clearly employers would be falling over themselves to offer me jobs.

But reality soon set in, and that didn't happen. Instead, I had to scramble and get something lined up. One of the best motivators I had for this was getting a job as a server/bartender: leave it to the service industry to really light a fire under you to seek out other employment. To be fair, we would be nowhere if we didn't have people doing these jobs, and I am forever grateful for them. As you'll learn later, I have had this odd pull back into this industry (via the "quick serve restaurant," or QSR, space) throughout my career, and it has led to me learning a lot more about the great people in that industry than I could have ever imagined.

A continuous job search finally landed me work as a software trainer at a software-training company. When I walked in for the interview, I was told I would need to come in to "present" in front of the executives that ran the company so they could see my presentation style and critique me.

I was very nervous, as most people would be at that age. Doing this really opened my eyes, however, in how best to present ideas in front of people. They recorded me in my faux "lesson" I'd had to learn about days prior, and it was amazing to see the amount of "ums" and "ands" that came out of my mouth. Hands down, it was one of the best experiences I could have had this early on in my career, and it really sharpened my presentation skills—along with being able to think on my feet. All this would really help me later as a consultant.

After interviewing/presenting to this company, I won the job. It was pretty stressful. You'd be handed a book on a certain tech that at the time you may have only known a little about: these were mainly covering the Microsoft office suite, but advancing into HTML or other coding, and all of the lessons were divided into the categories of beginner, intermediate and advanced.

The stressful part of this was mainly that you had to learn it very rapidly and then act really confident in front of the class, but that wasn't a huge problem as nine times out of ten they knew less than you—but there were the occasional smart people that just happened to know a *little* more than you.

It would be an understatement to say this really taught me how to think fast, act confident in my answer, and shift focus on the fly. I didn't realize then that doing this, even if only for a short while, would contribute so immensely to how I fashioned and approached my speaking style and practice. Now they call it things like "gravitas"; they say admiringly that speakers "have a smooth delivery and a personable style."

Back then, though, it was more like just survival of the fittest, and having knots in your stomach in the days and hours leading up to a class. On top of this difficulty, their classes were *long*—typically eight hours, so you really had to be "on" and deliver all day. This would contribute greatly to my strengths down the road, when I worked at Wharton and eventually consulted.

Quotas And Competition Force You To Develop Leadership Skills You Didn't Know You Needed

I was able to move on from the teaching job to find an account manager position at a Midwestern hardware and IT services company. It was based out of Chicago, and had a branch in Indianapolis. The people there were a real cast of characters—mostly crusty old vets from elsewhere in the industry. My job was to try to get people staffed at various companies to do IT-related jobs, as well as sniff out any large hardware opportunities. I was pretty junior, but leadership took a liking to me early on.

As this can remind us, it didn't start glamorous. I didn't have a clue to where my career was going to go, but it was helpful to see how hardware was (and still is) a part of this digital narrative. However, the lessons learned were a good starting point. I needed to hustle, had quotas and goals in sales, and it made me start to tap into the competitive and leadership qualities I had honed in sports in high shool and college to help give me a fighting chance. Those lessons would prove to be a good foundation to help me be successful in the short and long term along with helping me relate to and lead others.

Fear-Driven Markets Create Opportunity For Those Willing To Show Up

You young ones out there may need to look this one up, but in the years and months leading up to the year 2000, there was a lot of worry about what would happen with the world's computer systems and the industry at large. Floating around at that time was a kind of rumor that our computers wouldn't be able to comprehend the switch from the year 1999 to 2000.

It was supposed to be related to the first digit of the date changing from a one into a two: some systems were not thought to be programmed for this change, and certain commentators and specialists speculated they might attempt to default to the year 1900, 1000, or even *zero*.

In the computers' automated frenzy to cope with the current date suddenly predating their existence by decades or centuries, *everything* would supposedly break: planes would fall out of the sky, nuclear missiles would be rapid-fired from their siloes around the world, sewage pumps would flood Times Square in human waste; anything that could go wrong was projected to do exactly that, and mass hysteria and chaos would ensue. Some people were truly apocalyptic about it, and the major networks wouldn't stop talking about it—I'm sure they were loving it.

At the time, while I was with the IT staffing firm I mentioned, I happened to be on a big project with a large Midwestern insurance firm that was turning to a large consulting agency to help lead them through this (possible) crisis.

What did this mean for that consulting firm? Keep the fear-mongering going, and manage us contractors as we drove around the Midwest and slept at Holiday Inns (how fancy, brown-water coffee and cold continental breakfasts for everyone!), cataloging and updating each computer in their company with stickers that said they had either passed or failed inspection. This was my first exposure to a real "technology management consulting firm." They dressed nicer than us contractors, flew in and out every week, and *definitely* weren't staying at the Holiday Inns—but at some level, I could still relate to them and pick up on what they were talking about more easily than some of my colleagues, and sometimes even more so than the client.

I believed they noticed this and were quick to take me under their wings and assign me as the "leader." Did I get a raise or promotion for this? I don't think so. But it was sure thrilling to be in charge of a team that was going to help save companies from annihilation in the New Year!

And this did tap into a strength of mine, for sure: leading teams. Since I was young, I had always been a captain or leader of some sort on sports teams. The classroom was always another issue, but I took part in my fair share of clubs and so on. This and the benefit of having very social parents who forced me to think on my feet, be friendly and collegial in public settings—as well as to be open, honest and relatable—were the life skills I needed at an early age to help me in my career. I am grateful for them instilling that in me. It's paid dividends, for sure.

As for Y2K, the work itself was uneventful: the fun times on the road and bonding with colleagues are what I remember most. I remember driving from Indianapolis to Cincinnati with no air conditioning in the sweltering summer with the beater of a car I owned, the constant dinners at the old American family restaurant chains like Outback and Chili's along with all the other great American Midwest chain staples—and above all else, the beginning of my love/hate relationship with expense reports and time tracking!

Taking A Leap Before You're Ready Can Still Be The Right Move (Even If It Fails)

A dot-com company that sold and shipped unforgeable gift certificates was the company that Sean, my old water polo coach in college, convinced me to join.

The pluses were that it was a step up in opportunity in title and pay—it was funded—and he would be my boss. The minuses were that it was risky leaving my "sure thing" job and it required me being in Dayton every week away from home.

The dot-com thing was just so new—everyone wondered, could all these entrepreneurial companies dealing with the internet really be that successful? Thanks to the support of others and my wife at the time, I was encouraged to try it out. This would be my first entrepreneurial venture like this, and I had a mix of emotions. But (as my old water polo teammates would agree with me) I would follow my old coach into battle anywhere!

Sadly, it didn't last long. From what I remember, it was a whirlwind of about three months of up and down funding cycles, political backstabbing, Sean flying all over the country to get more funding, a trip with me to New York City (my first business one ever, which would foreshadow how many times I would be back) to pitch some companies where we ate in what was still a gritty Alphabet City (thanks Bill!), sat at communal tables at a restaurant (which was crazy for me: people in the big cities *did* this!?) and trying to get around Manhattan wearing a suit with a torrential downpour happening and getting absolutely soaked. Fun times—but it was very memorable.

🔑 Chapter Takeaways: Every Tech Panic Follows The Same Pattern—Learn It Now, Use It Forever

1. Every Era Has Its "WTF Is This?" Moment
   Whether it was IMs, HTML, or the first time someone said "Y2K," people have faced the frontier before. Generative AI is just the next wild frontier—and we are more prepared than we think. How you say? Whether it be leveraging fear for market opportunity, using soft skills to help open doors or saying yes before you fully feel ready, those lessons will help over time.

2. We've Been Training for This
   That feeling of faking it with just enough real knowledge to get by was my early software training. It sharpened my ability to think on my feet, lead a room, and stay ahead by staying engaged, which—funnily enough—are all skills that transfer directly to today's AI-fueled uncertainty.

3. I'm Not A Novice—I'm A Repeat Beginner
   I've started over before. I've left comfort zones, and I've said yes to long shots (even if they didn't pan out). An instinct for this is worth trusting now more than ever.

4. The Tech May Change—But Leadership Never Goes Out of Style
   From server installs to startup chaos, my ability to connect with people, rally teams, and lead through ambiguity became a real competitive edge. In the AI era, that edge gets even sharper.

5. Disruption = Innovation
   Every shift—the internet, Y2K, the dot-com boom—was both a threat and an opportunity. The same is true for AI. The question is: will you react, or will you lead?

6. It's Time To Pay It Forward
   Just like that professor who cracked open my digital mind, there are people right now waiting for me to help them make sense of what's next. Don't hoard your insight and experience. Use it.

7. History Doesn't Repeat—But It Does Rhyme
   My story—of curiosity, risk, and reinvention—is a blueprint. The details change, but the pattern is familiar. We can all lean into something like that with clear focus on what we're doing and courage.

CHAPTER 2

The Power of Being in the Right Place When Opportunity Doesn't Announce Itself

During our time in Indianapolis, my wife at the time was taking pre-MBA classes. She was very smart, and her outstanding scores on the GMAT test led her to apply to some of the best business schools of the time. Eventually, she was accepted into The Wharton School of the University of Pennsylvania in Philadelphia, and we moved there. I didn't know it at the time, but the University of Pennsylvania was the birthplace of the modern computer, 1945's ENIAC, which had apparently taken up 1,800 square feet when it was in use, and could perform up to 5,000 calculations per second. Perhaps this was fortuitous for me in some sense! As we visited Penn, I landed a job interview with the Executive Education part of Wharton. This would have been to help in an operations role to assist in the running of what was one of the great sources of income for the University. At the time, these top schools would sell out either custom (all people from the same company) or open enrollment (all seats sold to people from different companies) programs with the top professors to help generate revenue for the "non-profit" part of the University to help with research, recruiting top talent or upgrading the campus, etc.

My interview had started with a bang when my interviewer showed up, looked at me and told me, "Oh, Jamie? I thought you were a female!" This was before the days where you had to fill out any type of questionnaire that would designate such a thing when submitting a resume. But it didn't matter, and the interview went very well anyway; she liked me and I was hired. I ultimately worked at Penn for several years, and it was one of the most memorable, exciting, and glamorous (for a kid from Erie, Pennsylvania this was glamorous and exciting for me anyways) jobs I ever had. I got to travel the world, actually doing two whole contiguous round-the-world trips during it, and I saw quite a few top business luminaries speak. The colleagues and friendships I made there have lasted a lifetime.

Travel, Prestige, And Access To Power Teach You What Real Business Looks Like

Parenthetically, I think one could argue that after Covid, everything I describe in this sub-section has changed. What matters now is followers on LinkedIn, books, speaking and coaching engagements, and more. The world moves on, doesn't it? But let's continue:

During my time at Exec Ed, we had many big adventures. From having to straighten out the Finance group and trying to grow the business, to thinking through how you teach this product online—it was the early days of online learning! One of the biggest perks was getting to take courses and having access to the professors that even full-time MBA students didn't because A) those professors wanted to make more money and B) my leadership had the foresight to see that if I knew the product better, I could sell it better!

My boss Lynn was a great boss to work for. She was hard, but fair. She was also gracious with her time, but stern, and really held people to a higher standard. I had many great business trips with my colleagues to cities I had either never been to before—or only briefly and never really spent time there—like New York, Boston, Minneapolis, Chicago, and Los Angeles. I was getting to travel around the country and getting a feel for different cities and cultures, but I was also getting used to life on the road and what I would later realize was a taste of life as a consultant.

Some stories and lessons stand out to me from this time. The first was when my colleague Bill and I traveled from Philadelphia to Pittsburgh. As we stood there looking at the downtown skyline from Station Square, I mentioned how, having grown up in the small town of Erie, two hours north, this was always "the big city" to us. Bill, being from the Bronx, gave me a funny look and didn't stop laughing about it all day, and in fact often tells this story as a fond memory, even now. To me, though, it was the beginning of the realization that I had come a long way already from my modest upbringing in Erie, and at this point I was only 24 or 25 years old.

Another story that sticks with me from then was in Chicago. My colleague Jason and I finished some meetings early and some others had been cancelled, so we ended up with the afternoon free. This was before the time you would feel the angst to go somewhere, sit on your laptop and "get to work" or else feel guilty about not "working"—or, at least it was for me. Part of that may simply be that this was before laptops, though maybe we had a BlackBerry, but no matter. The situation was just that I was in Chicago, I had some free time, and I wanted to take the opportunity to see a Cubs game.

It took a little convincing by me to get Jason to blow off the afternoon, grab some last-minute outfield bleacher seats, have a few Old Style beers and enjoy the early summer sun. It was fantastic, and I'll never forget it, but unfortunately Jason was much higher up the totem pole than me, having other people that wanted or needed his time, and I remember him being a bit stressed after the game—he had to call some people back and work on proposals. This was a realization to me that the higher you climb in the corporate world, the more demands are put on your time, and the more expectations rise.

It wouldn't be until many years later I would realize this, but regardless, I always *tried* to mix pleasure with business. I always thought, if there was no way to at least have a little pleasure involved while on the road away from home, what would be the point of anything?

And as an aside, that single experience bonded me and Jason more than any other "work thing" we ever did together. It's good to be friends with your collaborators, and having a little fun is the way to that.

9/11: Many Personal Moments That Marked My Time During It

9/11. I will never forget where I was, and what happened, on this day. As we were kicking off our programs with various executive teams and companies, I settled in with the rest of the admin staff for work in the back office when over the cubicles I started to hear murmurs that a plane had hit one of the twin towers. That was like my back yard: New York is just a short Amtrak ride from Philly, really.

Given that I was on the East Coast, as well as the amount of New Yorkers at the University of Pennsylvania, this caused significant interest and concern. I remember that a group of us ended up in the classroom of a custom exec course being taught to executives visiting from Germany. The professor put the live news up on the large screen at the front of the classroom and we all watched in horror as a second plane crashed into the *other* building on live television.

None of us could believe—or even comprehend—what we had really seen. The executives visiting from Germany started leaving the room and calling loved ones, knowing they'd be stuck in the US for a while. Our staff was dismissed early, the school closed for the day, and those of us that could, not knowing what would happen next, walked home. I lived at the time in a high-rise in the Center City neighborhood of Philadelphia—which, being next to the two tallest buildings in the city, didn't exactly feel great. We walked around Center City, got together with friends at a local Italian restaurant, and tried to process what we had seen and what had happened while the events were broadcast on replay, over and over again, on the TV above the bar. It was an unreal day, and still tattooed into my brain.

Moving From The "Sure Thing" At Exec Ed To The Entrepreneurial Digital Startup For Wharton: Knowledge@Wharton

It's scary to leave a cash cow, but it's thrilling to take on a new venture. This would define my career in ways you'll see later on. After I had been at Exec Ed only about a year, little did I know that the person who would be my future boss, Mukul, had earlier been brought in to Wharton and then asked to think of a way for Wharton to get their thought leadership out into the world. Harvard had long been doing so through their powerful *Harvard Business Review*—that magazine with very lengthy articles that all business executives liked to leave on their coffee tables or desks to look smart. We called it the "coffee table book" because that's usually where you could find it, and we were convinced it was rarely picked up.

It was around the year 1998 when Mukul had amazing foresight to suggest that Wharton *not* do a magazine like Harvard—which I believe was what leadership was thinking they wanted—but, rather, fully embrace the digital aspect in the new world we were finding ourselves in and publish the articles online and then just e-mail out a summary every two weeks. I don't remember all the specifics, as I was still working in Exec Ed, but I am sure it was a very uphill battle for Mukul to try to convince leadership that this was the best way forward. The genius of the product was that it would be relevant, somewhat timely (not a daily post, but at least refreshed every two weeks), lengthy but not as lengthy as a Harvard or Economist article, and incorporate the faculty at Wharton representing the academic side while also including people in business who could provide more depth with their views in practice.

I credit our leader at Exec Ed, Bob, for seeing this vision and realizing it would be something that had a lot of potential. I also credit him for giving the green light and supporting it for as long as he did. It wasn't easy to be funding something like this when people had to be convinced of the value all the time; I'm sure he got a lot of heat.

Early Stage Startups Need Sales More Than They Need Strategy (And Sales People Know It)

Knowledge@Wharton needed some help when it came to sales and marketing. I'm not sure how or why my name ever ended up being mentioned in conversation, but it was presented to me to see if I wanted to help with that and at least split my time in the beginning. I met with Mukul, liked the vision, liked how it was different and really liked the entrepreneurial aspect of it. It was like joining a startup with a really rich uncle—which, incidentally, was a phrase I would find myself using often in my career and for the roles/opportunities I typically found myself interviewing for. I was excited, and looked forward to the challenges and opportunities up the road!

🔑 Chapter Takeaways: From Ivory Tower To Entrepreneurial Edge

1. Sometimes, The Path Finds You
   A spontaneous job interview—a misunderstood first name—or a move for someone else's dream. Often, the most important parts of your story don't arrive through perfect planning, but through being open and willing to move forward (or sideways, as the case may sometimes also be).

2. You Learn The Most When You're Closest To The Action
   Whether wrangling finance teams, traveling for exec programs, or sneaking off to a Cubs game, real-world exposure shaped my instincts. The core was direct contact with how people work, live, and lead.

3. Glamour And Grit Can Coexist
   From travel and Ivy League prestige to watching 9/11 unfold from a classroom, I lived an unusual professional life of high-touch business in a high-stakes world. That duality gave me a deeper kind of presence and purpose.

4. Entrepreneurship Isn't Always a Leap; Sometimes It's More Of A Slide
   I didn't quit everything and start from scratch. I followed a pull, accepted a challenge, and moved from a "cash cow" to an unproven thing. This is what happens when you combine a little bit of guts with a clear idea.

5. Being Early Requires Conviction And A Sales Mindset
   Knowledge@Wharton wasn't obvious. But I saw the play, believed in the team, and stepped into the role: go get money, go make it real. That's what entrepreneurs do—sell the future before others believe it.

CHAPTER 3

Building Thought Leadership Before "Thought Leadership" Was Even a Thing

Selling Something New Means Selling An Idea, Not Just A Product

In the beginning, many of us in the digital sales and advertising space were going through the challenge of how to get money from companies to help fund these entrepreneurial digital ventures. It was tough going. Us sales people were tasked with walking into a company and convincing them of the breadth and depth of our product along with the reach it had with consumers.

It was all about the impressions—but what do I mean by that? Well, once you got the meeting secured, they actually *showed up to meet*. Back then, meeting in person was the only way, kids. No Zoom, or even phone calls. You would go through your sales pitch, they would politely (in most cases) nod and ask a few questions, then you would take a big gulp and share what the cost was to have their company's logo be "privileged" enough to be able to grace the home page (and later every other page) of our great thought leadership website from *the* Wharton School: Knowledge@Wharton (insert your own digital property here.)

I don't remember the specifics, but do remember it was a smaller number—maybe around $50-100k—in the beginning when we were just getting started, and became bigger, going to $200-300k over time as we grew. The sales pitch was the "impressions" our site got, and the distribution and prestige of having their logo associated with the Wharton brand. It was the same thing the *Harvard Business Review* was doing, but in a digital form.

This was in the first real heyday of online advertising, and the whole industry was trying to figure out how to quantify the value of having a "clickable logo" on a website—*and* this was before Google or the other search engines were mature enough, save one big one that we'll get to next. Ad agencies were also trying to figure out the large media companies.

Though the first person in my life to have a big impact on the way I approached sales was Sean, I would be remiss if I didn't talk about another person: Bruce. I was pulled into a meeting one day with Mukul while I was hustling at Knowledge@Wharton where he told me on the spot that we were about to be having a call with a veteran Silicon Valley man. There weren't many of these at the time: to call him a "vet" in 2001 also probably meant he'd been there from the start, and was soon going to *leave*, too. (You might compare that to the careerists who would always be there.)

In any case, Bruce explained to us on the ensuing call that he was a Penn/Wharton alum, having become successful in sales on the East Coast in New York/New Jersey for a telecom company over the course of many years, then risked it all and took a chance by joining a Silicon Valley startup that dealt with online auctions. He had been a very early employee there and had helped build the charity arm of their business—auctioning off signed paraphernalia, for example, to be bid on for charity.

Of course, eBay became hugely successful, and is still with us today without having hardly changed at all. Despite that, at the time of this call, he wanted to leave it and help his alma mater advance in the business world (as well as travel the world and make money for them).

To give context for myself, here I was, a kid from a small town in Pennsylvania from a blue collar family, whose parents had worked for the same companies their whole lives and couldn't understand why I wasn't doing that—I was already on my third employer since graduating college four years earlier—and here was this man who'd basically done so well that he could just walk away from his employer, take a *huge* pay cut by moving to Penn, and dedicate his work life to that while having kids and living in one of the most expensive zip codes in the country at the time.

I couldn't wrap my head around it. I thought there was a catch. But there wasn't; it turns out that this was just a world I'd had no idea existed. And I'd be learning a lot more about it, because I was about to go on the road with Bruce.

Parenthetically, this also spoke to how we'd always been taught to work hard for our whole lives and strive for the next promotion or raise without ever thinking we could do well enough to take bigger risks later in our careers (or even just be encouraged and supported to take risks like that earlier regardless), or have the space to do more of what we wanted to do rather than what our employer thought we should do.

I clearly remember my first time meeting Bruce in person and going on a sales trip to New York with him. I worked pretty hard to get meetings set up with some very well-known Wall Street firms. When I took the train up to meet Bruce, he told me to meet him at the building of one of them in Manhattan, and he'd be wearing a sport coat and a Wharton shirt. This was in a time where I was wearing suits for meetings, as many were in those days (except when hitting the West Coast, where the form was to ditch the tie and downgrade to a sport coat and slacks). So, when he said this, I didn't really process the odd note of "Wharton shirt". I showed up fresh off the Amtrak in my best dark blue Wall Street suit and found Bruce in a sport coat, blue Wharton T-shirt with the logo prominently displayed on the chest, light-colored jeans, and... hiking boots. I was horrified. But I kept my mouth shut, reasoning that here was a very successful sales person active on both the East and West coasts with a Wharton degree. What did I know?

We had our meetings with what I believe were some odd looks from the folks in those buildings, and had essentially zero wins over the course of the day. After it was all over, Bruce smiled and said he guessed he should've worn a suit. Yeah, Bruce. Next time you're on Wall Street, maybe wear the suit. But I was glad we could joke about it and still do to this day.

The Friction Of Pre-GPS Travel Taught Me More About Resilience Than Comfort Ever Could

In the early days, I was on the road, trying to drum up business, and spent a lot of time in San Francisco and Silicon Valley. I loved it: it was sort of a Golden Age, and like the Wild West out there. Anything seemed to go. I'd book meetings in the Valley and downtown, but I'd always try to stay downtown when I could—which meant I spent a lot of time back and forth on Route 101, an infamous stretch of highway that, at the time, though very busy, was not as busy as it was about to get when the Valley really took off. At the time we didn't have GPS or Google Maps, and I'd have to do the unbelievably tedious thing compared to today and plan out the routes and directions through an early website called MapQuest, print out the directions, then try to read them line-by-line while driving the 101 at various speeds. Nothing recalculated if you missed your turn; it could be a little nerve-wracking. No matter what I did, even when trying to drive at low-traffic hours, there never seemed to be a perfect time to go. It blew my mind the pure *scale* of things: all the people, all the cars and trucks, all the *lanes* that were just dedicated to keeping people moving along that route. Sure, there was also a light rail, but that didn't help when you needed to visit lots of offices in a single day and there wasn't the convenience of Uber or Lyft. You needed a car and your trusty MapQuest directions.

Most Ambitious People Choose The Obvious Path (Which Is Why The Unconventional Path Has Less Competition)

The graduating Master of Business Administration scene in America in 2003 looked like this: a majority of students angling for investment banking, consulting, or tech in Silicon Valley. It seemed those were the main three choices. Maybe that's not so surprising, considering these were all type-A Wharton MBAs. It was all about maximizing value and getting return on that *huge* investment just made into a career pivot, or that next notch in the belt in order to get promoted and someday be the one with the corner office.

These people did *not* lack ambition. This was during a not-so-great financial situation in the US that, while not like the 2008 crisis, wasn't really great, so it felt good or lucky to even have jobs lined up. There weren't a lot of students going to "startups" or joining non profit entities, it seemed. It was more risk and less reward in terms of paycheck. But the stories of time spent at the office for all the big three industry people seemed like hell: I heard countless stories of our Wall Street friends having to wait at the office all day until the bosses got out of their meetings and gave the recent MBA grads, who they treated more like lackeys than anything, their assignments to work on all evening. "Sure, you can order dinner in and have black car service home on us: just don't leave the office until it's done." That would often mean 2-4am in the morning, and sometimes not at all. How did these "kids" function like this? Consulting was only slightly better, but hey, it meant more travel and racking up those frequent flier miles and hotel points, at least. Given my line of work at the time, I was exposed to all of this. What I could say was that it seemed like those going into tech had more risk involved, but at least a somewhat better lifestyle—though I am sure many were working those hours and disagree with me!

Yahoo Was King—At First

It feels weird to say or write in 2025, but it was true. During my early days in the tech industry, Yahoo was the largest search engine around. If you needed something, you used Yahoo, and for cultural cachet, Yahoo was where it was at. My friend Brian, who I met at Wharton, worked for them—so given that, and that we often met with some Wharton alumni who were there in prominent positions, it was the search company I had the most experience with at the time. That wouldn't last for too long, though.

Visiting Google In The Early Days

At some point, I ended up on a trip with Mukul and Bruce where we would be joining a marketing professor from Wharton while he held meetings and a lecture at a very small search engine company located in an old corporate strip, one-story building right on the 101 with the strange name of Google. You might imagine what the explanation at the time was of what Google did: they were trying to be Yahoo, but smaller. I don't remember much of the meeting or lecture, but I do clearly remember that Google was small enough at the time to only take up one floor, and only had around a thousand employees. I also distinctly remember one of the employees gleefully telling us that they had, of all people, the chef for the Grateful Dead slinging tacos out in their quad. Was *this* the company's claim to fame?

eBay

At some point, Bruce and I visited eBay on our own. Compared to Yahoo and Google, eBay seemed to be way more established—and, I'm guessing at the time, a way easier business model to grasp. eBay was pretty straightforward. It was online auctions, or the electronic version of a literally ancient way of buying and selling, versus whatever-the-hell techno-mumbo-jumbo a "search engine" was. What was that supposed to do, or how would it make money? This was the early days of trying to figure out search engines and how they could actually turn a profit. That wasn't really happening yet, and it was long before something like Google AdWords became big.

Bruce obviously still had connections there: I recall that former eBay luminaries were always asking Bruce to help support their latest political or philanthropic ventures. Nothing big from the meetings stands out, but I do remember sitting outside having lunch with Bruce at eBay when he introduced me to the janitor. I said hello, he said hello back, he was very gracious and nice, and then took his leave of us. Bruce then told me the janitor had been with eBay at the beginning and they've given him some stock. I was doing the math on what *any* amount of early stock might be worth by then—surely it was gigantic—when Bruce delivered the coup de grace: "Jamie, how many janitors do you know who go to Hawaii four times a year?"

Again: a different time.

Seeing Breakthrough Technology Early Doesn't Mean You'll Understand Its Impact (Or Act On It)

Another big thing for us was our trip to Seattle to meet with Microsoft and Amazon. These were two of the more established companies during the early 2000s in the tech (that is, pre-"digital") space. The highlights of the trip included a moment where I saw Jeff Bezos at a Starbucks in downtown Seattle while drinking coffee with Bruce and Mukul. Mukul could barely hold his excitement as he whispered and pointed him out to me. Bezos wasn't yet the tech-world god he is today—and this was so long ago now that he actually had hair! Though I didn't talk to him, I can at least say I saw him once. Even so, I thought it was cool he was out having a meeting at a coffee shop rather than at his office—embracing that now-ubiquitous work-from-anywhere mentality, certainly.

For my part, I was learning and adapting to doing business outside of the office, which was still a newer concept—or at least one that wasn't as prevalent outside of sales at the time, or so it seemed to me. It could have just been my experience, but we didn't have the technology (or employer mentality) to free us from our desks as much. The iPhone wouldn't come out for several more years.

The other big part of that road trip was our time at Amazon HQ where we met an Amazon executive that was dealing with content for Amazon. We were (or at least Mukul was) trying to pitch them on content co-creation or sharing. Bruce and I were angling for money.

So this Amazon executive pulls us into a room, then tells us we need to sign an NDA before we can proceed. I was young, and this was the first time I ever had to do this, so I didn't know what to think, but after talking about it for a moment I followed Mukul and Bruce's lead and we all signed it.

The Amazon executive then brings in a very early prototype of something he called a Kindle. We got to hold it, play with it and ask *lots* of questions about it. It may seem hard to believe now, but it was hugely groundbreaking at the time—a way to replace books and magazines with a physical tech product that delivered text content in a digital form. This was basically a first in this field: there were no iPads yet, and the PalmPilot was just for note taking and very basic functionality. We were floored to hear about the plans and ambition.

And they wanted to partner with us to deliver K@W content!

A Top Strategy Firm: Some Client Relationships Span Decades And Teach You Everything About Industry Evolution

Early on at K@W we had several anchor clients, and they were all fantastic. It was interesting selling for a higher-ed institution versus a consulting firm or business. It seemed that people were more willing to meet with us, especially with a brand name like Wharton behind us. One of the industries we got a lot of attention from was consulting firms. And why not? They had lots of our alumni, with all of them trying to establish their own brands and thought leadership while building the brand of their own firms. We had the big three consulting firms working with us, who some people refer to as "MBB"(McKinsey, Bain and BCG, or Boston Consulting Group), and paying us a good amount of money to be there. A company that sticks out in my memory, and perhaps the one we had the deepest relationship with, was one of these MBB firms. The whole MBB world was new to me at this time; in fact, all of "consulting" was. But clearly I saw the difference between Deloitte and Accenture vs. an MBB firm—it was evident in the offices alone. This company was on Park Avenue; that's never *not* been a big deal.

The two people we met with the most were running the marketing and advertising budget for the firm. They were great to work with and bounce ideas off, and they always had time for us. They also helped push K@W to new areas of content development and partnership models—it was all about the co-branded thought leadership back then (and it really still is in some cases). I learned a lot from them, additionally, about the publishing world, and the brand-building one can do by getting something like articles and books out there. Remember, again, that this predated podcasting. I really enjoyed working with this MBB company, and it turned out to be the start of a 25-year relationship in which I'd be selling to them, working for them, and then eventually working *with* and selling *back* to them.

Patience Is A Virtue: A Valuable Lesson?

During my time on the road with Bruce, one of the biggest sales lessons I learned was with a major South Korean consumer electronics company that shall go unnamed.

Bruce and I had secured a meeting with a VP of marketing for the company right in New Jersey, outside of New York City. We drove up there and proceeded to wait in the lobby for this VP—but he made us wait, and wait, and then wait even more. After nearly an hour and a half, the VP of marketing walked in and asked the admin if he missed anything. When she told him we were waiting for him he turned, looked at us, didn't acknowledge us at all, then walked back into his office.

Of course, I'm thinking: what did I just *see*? Furious, I told Bruce we should leave, but he calmed me down and asked the admin to call the VP again to ask if we could meet. They said he would see us, but then he made us wait even *more*. Finally, he let us into his office.

He was there with a few other people, and asked us with some disinterest what it was that we wanted. After such a series of snubs, suddenly Bruce turned into an unstoppable machine. Looking back, I don't remember saying a single thing during the meeting. He launched into how excellent our website and newsletter were, how many impressions we were getting, the prestigious companies that already had their logos on our site, and so on. This was usually a back-and-forth with me and Bruce to the person we were selling to, but not today. Bruce was in the driver's seat on this one, and wasn't going to take no for an answer. I remember the conversation between this person and Bruce. It went from the practical hostility of the VP saying "you have to be kidding me, I'm in the wrong business" to Bruce *getting behind the VP's desk with him*, looking at his computer, explaining the product and promotion, and then the VP telling his staff to come over to look.

After all the strange antipathy the VP had shown, followed by Bruce's incredible work, we walked out of that office with a $300,000 commitment. It seemed like the right salesperson—Bruce, in this case—could literally sell ice to Eskimos.

I couldn't believe the turnaround. It was *truly* impressive, and taught me a lot about patience and not taking no for an answer, even if my approach happens to be slightly different from Bruce's.

Bruce became one of my biggest inspirations, but I've met many other excellent sales people that have taught me things like this over the years. They are all exceptional, and I am inspired by them every time I think about them.

From Sean, to Bruce, to many others, the sales people that can quickly learn the product, create a very compelling narrative around it, package it and sell it are the ones that can excel, hit goals and truly master what they do. Especially if they can do it without coming off as a cheesy used car salesman. The art of learning and mastering the field of consultative sales, turning something ambiguous into something clear and showing the true value of the product, is what's really important. Asking open-ended questions, active listening, and being very likeable and relatable are key components and skills to master to become more successful in sales—and I've seen it live, from some of the best.

Podcasting?

I will definitely credit Mukul for being a visionary in many things, but sticking with podcasting has to be one of the biggest. At the time, I didn't understand it: who would want to listen to people drone on about business topics rather than just read it online? Well, like many things, I was wrong. Looking back on it now, it was foolish *not* to believe in it. Especially in this day and age when normal people all over the world seem to be running podcasts about practically anything, and the way people also can read books in the "listening" form of an audiobook.

Hell, you have people and celebrities now inking multimillion dollar deals for *their* podcasts—looking at you, Kelce Brothers and Smartless crew. The early days of it involved setting up multiple microphones in Mukul's office, making sure nobody disturbed the recording, and accidentally catching the sounds coming through the windows at the University of Pennsylvania's Steinberg Dietrich Hall. The beauty of it was you could then turn your interviews into long-form articles so people could choose how they wanted to consume it. Though the podcast started off modestly, it grew rapidly in terms of downloads. Being at a university like Penn was great because as we grew, more of the school took notice, which led to more important guests for our shows.

Traveling The World For Knowledge@Wharton

Taking that leap to K@W also helped me see the world. After a few years of success—though it never really felt like it, it seemed that even with sponsorships we were always asking the University for more money—we made the decision to launch versions of K@W in Spain, India and China. This meant working with local teams in those countries and having many meetings and attending alumni events there. Some of the highlights included traveling to Madrid for meetings with our main sponsor, Banco Santander, where everyone smoked in the office. This was the first time I ever "worked from the hotel" in my life (thanks to me wanting to avoid all the smoke) and would be a precursor for many "work from hotel" times once I got into consulting.

After this, another glamorous thing (the former, not the latter, as you will see) was staying at the Taj Mahal Palace Hotel in Mumbai and eating at the Leopold Cafe only months after it had been the center of a terrorist attack. I shudder to think what would have happened if I'd been in that hotel at the time and answered the door when the terrorists were going around.

CHAPTER 3

Finally, there was China, where things definitely felt more foreign, and where you absolutely needed to know someone high up to get anything done. I also remember the time I showed up there and my luggage had not, and I was due to meet the mayor of Shanghai the next day. I was whisked away by an assistant we were working with down some back alley in Shanghai, and in less than 24 hours I had a custom-made suit. It was unreal—but that was just how my life was at the time.

Working at Wharton was one of the best, and most formative, parts of my career. It taught me invaluable lessons and helped shape me into who I am now, and I look back fondly on it.

Moving Closer To Home And The First Foray Into Remote Work!

During this time we welcomed our first born son into this world, Kyle. It was exciting and scary at the same time. He suffered jaundice for a bit and there was a minor scare that he might have to go back into the hospital, but after many hours with a UV machine wrapped around him, countless hours spent sleeping on the couch with him, and actually placing him in the windowsill of our Philadelphia home so he could get natural UV rays, he got better. It was during this time we realized how much we missed being by family and the tremendous help it would be being near them while we both pursued and managed our career aspirations. So during this time we decided to move to Pittsburgh to be closer to family—this being a two-hour drive to Cleveland and Erie rather than the seven- to eight-8 hour drive.

The biggest question for me and the conversation with work I was most nervous about was whether Mukul would be okay with me working "remotely". A few factors that I think helped make his agreement easier were the rise of laptops and BlackBerrys, more accessible internet access and technology in general, and people beginning to realize you could work "anywhere". Not that this was necessarily a good thing, as we would see with so many burnt-out career-chasing professionals later.

Also helpful: Southwest Airlines flights coming into the Pittsburgh and Philadelphia airports that dropped airfare so much you could do a roundtrip (30 minutes in the air, if even that) for around $150. Those were East Corridor Amtrak prices! Anyway, I was traveling a lot already for work to other locations outside of Philadelphia, so what did it matter where I sat? True, there was less opportunity to have face-to-face meetings and less "face time" with key admin people, but hell, I was selling for them. The less time there meant more time I was out selling.

With Mukul's blessing, we packed our Honda CRV to the brim (the rest handled by movers, as Kyle's mom was able to secure a great job with a big pharma company in Pittsburgh that paid for the move) with only barely enough room for Kyle and the dog and we headed off to Pittsburgh.

The early days of trying to "work from home" while managing Kyle as he was too young to be in school yet were at times frustrating, but still worth it. I remember this feeling of trying to keep him by my desk playing (while not napping) while I would frantically keep an eye on my laptop, manage emails, expense reports, work calls etc. Looking back on it, even though I made it work, and it was great to spend the time with him, I should have done a better job "time boxing" certain aspects of it. I should've dedicated time to be more present with him and balanced that better with the needs of work. There is no need to be hovering over a laptop, *ever*, if there is nothing of value being done/added. It was still good bonding time I got to spend with him at an early age, though, and clearly I had very few peers that were managing a career this way—if any, and especially male—so it felt groundbreaking to me at the time. Eventually the travel and time away from home began to wear on me, and decisions had to be made about career growth, income, life, and so on, which led me to interview for more local jobs where I could still pursue digital work and grow my career in that area.

🔑 Chapter Takeaways: Digital Sales And Dot-Com Chaos: Early Career Mentors Shape Your Definition Of What's Possible

1. Being Early Means Being Misunderstood
   "You want me to pay *what* to put a logo on your site?" Selling digital value before the market truly grasped it taught you to explain, persuade, and stick through disbelief—and these are critical muscles in every emerging wave, from the early internet to AI.

2. Presence Is More Important Than Polish
   From hiking boots on Wall Street to Grateful Dead tacos at Google, I learned that authenticity builds trust—and that reading the room is more important than fitting a mold.

3. Mentorship Can Be A Masterclass
   Bruce was both a major sales mentor for me and a window into a world I hadn't imagined yet. To watch him operate, recover from a snub, and close a $300K deal taught me that resilience plus narrative equaled influence.

4. Ask Questions, Test Limits, Translate For Others
   I saw tech history up close and kept my eyes open. From early Google and Amazon to podcasting, I found myself exposed to some of the most important early innovations in the modern tech world. I asked questions, tested limits, and translated it for others. You can go far with this beginner's mindset, even when witnessing history.

5. Sales Is Persuasion And Evangelism
   I was selling impressions or logos, but what I was really selling was ideas: in media shifts, in brand alignment, and in new ideas themselves. It turned pitches into partnerships with firms as large as the MBB organizations.

6. Get Permission For Work-Life Experiments First, Then Set Boundaries
   My early foray into remote work with a newborn taught me what most only discovered years later: flexibility doesn't mean much if you aren't careful with how you organize your time. Once you get permission for hybrid work, you've got to balance it carefully.

7. The Road Was My Classroom
   Madrid, Mumbai, Shanghai, Seattle—I learned a lot here selling globally and adapting locally. I built cross-cultural skills that would define my career's next phases, and I'd recommend it to you, too.

CHAPTER 4

When Your Integrity Costs You a Paycheck—And Why Walking Away Without a Plan Can Actually Work

Managing Demanding Clients Teaches You More Than Any Training Program

I managed to get an offer with a small digital agency around 2009. I was brought on as an account manager at a company where they wanted me to manage a big university client: both the main and the business school. With my background, I was a perfect choice. The school? Carnegie Mellon and the Tepper School of Business. It's one of the preeminent tech, science and robotics-based universities in the world. I quickly learned that, unfortunately, I would be working with one of the most demanding clients I'd ever had. These were the type of people that if you didn't answer the phone, or call back, it immediately triggered a chain of phone calls to upper management on why you weren't being responsive enough: brutal. I *was* able to manage it, though, and also had a great mentor in Steve who helped show me the ropes and started me out learning how to think more strategically. I found I appreciated his laid-back, calm approach, which was definitely in line with mine. He taught me a lot, and was great to have meetings and share meals with.

The job didn't last too long, but one of the important things I did here was stick to the values my parents taught me and kept my integrity even at this crazy startup agency. At a certain point I learned I wouldn't be getting the bonus I was promised when I was hired, and I quickly made an exit plan and started interviewing elsewhere, segueing pretty neatly into a for-profit higher education company that was big and happened to be headquartered in Pittsburgh.

For-Profit Higher Ed Digital Landscape

The "Other Side" Of Education

I had almost no exposure to the for-profit higher education industry at this point; I hadn't even known it existed! It was dominated by the University of Phoenix, Devry, and others. Though I never felt great about their tactics, one thing I did see them embrace and perfect more than non-profits was the use of digital content and tools, from both an enrollment and education standpoint. Online learning, for example: I'd seen Wharton try and fail at this multiple times, though with a few successes. The adoption rates just hadn't been there, and at the time it seemed clear that people wouldn't or couldn't focus and succeed outside a classroom as much as inside one. You might say there was a similar arc compared to working from home.

Looking back, those failed attempts at online learning were dress rehearsals for what we're seeing now with AI in education. Back then, we couldn't crack the code on engagement and quality. But now there are AI tutors, personalized learning paths, instant feedback on study exercises that actually helps the learner—it's everything we *dreamed* about in 2002 but couldn't build. The difference is that this time the technology is actually caught up to the vision. Though I still see universities making the same mistake: focusing on the tech instead of asking what problem they're actually trying to solve.

The company I joined was led by some former University of Phoenix executives and seemed to be trying to copy their model. They owned four university systems, teaching subjects ranging from arts, to business, to nursing, and mixes of all of the above, and tried to embrace where people were going online, as well as diving into the data and strategy to enroll people online, which would ultimately realize big cost savings over in-person enrollment, especially when done at volume. They were also, of course, marketing more flexibility over traditional education as "online learning" began to take the forms we associate with it today. I became Senior Director of Digital, which led me to Bob, the "Godfather of B2B commerce"—his words, not mine—which would play a *huge* role in my career trajectory. There'll be more to come on that.

A group of us under Bob's leadership would be the "digital brand directors" for each of the universities. The culture was interesting, as a lot of new people were being hired very rapidly. I believe the company had just received a big round of funding to "catch up" with University of Phoenix, which at the time was something like the industry's 800-pound-gorilla. We led and managed everything: website redesigns, digital marketing, and SEO/SEM strategies. When I think about it now, it wasn't the most exciting or glamorous work, but it did help me start out in the digital space beyond just sales or marketing, and would set my knowledge base for what eventually would lead to a path into consulting.

Discovery Of A/B Testing And The Power Of Simple Changes

One of the tactics we were deeply exploring at the time was A/B testing. This was a practice of having one design or one sample of copy compete against another one, either vastly or slightly different. We did a lot of this back then and the data helped us make a myriad of decisions, like using a blue versus red button on a webpage, or using longer, more detailed copy on another one, and so on. It really helped us make decisions based on data and, consequently, we typically saw increased enrollment numbers.

We thought this was pretty sophisticated, but it took a lot of manual work. In the past you would test things like colors, copy or banners, etc. It then progressed to slightly more complicated "person-alization" where you could tie in constructed experiences like images or the previous things I mentioned based on location, industry, and so on. It's sped up in the past few years, even before LLMs, but now I watch companies use AI to run thousands of micro-experiments simultaneously and personalize experiences for each user in real-time. The thing that hasn't changed is you still need to know why you're testing and what you're optimizing for. The tools got smarter, but you've still got to be strategic.

"Just Make Sure It Doesn't Suck," Or The Building Of A Website In 2008-2010: Perfectionism Kills More Projects Than Bad Ideas Do

We had a team of hard-working developers and designers, and it was always an interesting journey to work to create these digital prop-erties and assets. It wasn't as structured as what I would experience once I started consulting more heavily in the space, and it was like a ballet within a large orchestrated dance number to get the products live. What now takes days or weeks would take months then. There would be the strategy work behind it, working with the agencies to define it more, look at designs, then bridge that gap with the agency's work and feeding that into the development team.

This is where my role would be the most important: that transla-tion from the agency to the internal developers and coders, who were always leery of the type of assets and work the agencies did for us. I think it was in their nature. One clear example I remember from this was a back-and-forth between me and a developer on a certain design asset from our agency. At some point after endless dialogue about what was exactly being asked for—I swear, these developers had past lives as lawyers, there was so much ass-covering—I finally told him in front of both his boss and a roomful of developers to "just make sure it doesn't suck".

I would find I would use this phrase a lot more later on in my digital career: simple and direct works. In this case, it had come to the point to be direct—but I was also pushing back on the sadly-common tendency of hiding behind requirements to avoid making mistakes or being blamed for problems. Putting this man suddenly in charge of solving the problem *solved the problem*: it was done surprisingly fast, and exceptionally well. He stopped letting perfect get in the way of good enough.

Another lesson here is that empowering and enabling non-creative people to own the creative process, instead of letting them shrink away from it, can lead to great results.

There's A Price For Selling Something You Don't Believe In, And It's Higher Than The Salary

After some time, I started picking up on clues that would lead me to quit for-profit school work. I heard rumblings of strongarm tactics to get students enrolled, similar to the way armed services sometimes recruited kids. I heard that the company was leveraging the government's loan model to get more money, and that the school facilities were often pretty empty or generally lacking in necessary materials. The list of problems continued while these people were trying to keep costs as low as possible. It was despicable behavior, to use a strong word that still seems to fit. I saw this first-hand on some roadtrips to schools where we were looking to understand more. What I thought would be trips to meet administration and students turned into fielding complaints and gripes, mainly by students, on the lack of things like Wi-Fi, fellow students who couldn't read or write and were dragging the classes down, and the school administration positioning itself for more funds from the government.

Getting the government to prop up the industry with our tax dollars seemed to be the strategy of these for-profit institutions—and the ship suddenly looked like it was about to start going down during the Obama administration when the government finally understood all the money it was sending to students for student aid was being handed right over to the for-profits.

While I think it had been helpful to have alternatives to expensive non-profit institutions, and it did a lot of good for some people, the media was beginning to cover it more and I was getting so aware of these ugly practices of recruitment, enrollment and the education itself that I had to get out.

Apart from my own hesitation, the government clearly was starting to see that it had to re-assess the whole school-funding model, but this wasn't why I decided to leave: I just came to the realization myself that this for-profit school was no University of Pennsylvania or Wharton, and I couldn't stand the "product" we were helping put out to do what was, in the end, something like take advantage of these students. It felt bad and wrong that the management and the school administrations seemed to be fine with it. I'm sure there are two sides to every story, but it didn't meet the standard I had in my mind for the core beliefs and values I had around education. Though with perspective now, one could argue the non-profits (even the Ivy Leagues) have started going this route with enormous tuition bills, administrative staffing costs, and grift. We are now in a time where undergrad and graduate educations are being called out for how much "value" they give people who pursue those degrees—given their enormous costs.

The for-profit education disaster I saw feels eerily relevant now as every educational startup says they'll "revolutionize learning with AI." It's the same breathless promises and focus on profitability over usefulness. The technology is infinitely better now, because AI *can* actually deliver personalized education at scale, but the basic question remains: are we using this to genuinely educate people, or just to extract the most revenue with the least effort? I've seen this movie before, and I know how it ends when it plays out like that.

So I decided to leave.

Walking Away Without A Backup Plan Is Always An Option

In hindsight, I could have handled the leaving much better. But if I had, then maybe I wouldn't have ended up where I am. I remember after weeks/months of back-and-forth internally, I decided I was going to quit. I don't remember much discussion with my then-wife about it, but I clearly remember the look of shock and total disbelief on her face when I said I wanted to leave without having another job lined up. Knowing what I know now, this was totally reasonable, as we were both brought up to follow the default path: school, followed by jobs, maybe followed by grad school, then keep climbing that ladder. At this point, I'm not sure what the deciding factor was, or if it was just the constant pit in my stomach of waking up every day to commute in to try to peddle more of this product that was taking advantage of people and using our tax dollars to do it. But it was time for me to stand up for what I believed and move on.

I remember some conversation that went something like: " I'll just be a stay-at-home Dad and figure it out." It wasn't a very deeply-thought-out plan, I just knew I needed to get out, and I'm still thankful to my then-wife for being so supportive, even if she probably thought I was insane and would never amount to anything if this was to be my course of action (which would have been fair) as I started this new journey. But, thankfully, this transitional period didn't last long.

Your Network Can Find You When You're Visible About Needing Help: The Power Of LinkedIn

The People Who Know Your Real Value Will Reach Out When You Need Them Most

I clearly remember updating my LinkedIn profile to "independent consultant," which you could probably equate to that LinkedIn designation of "open to work" now. There wasn't too much going into LinkedIn strategy back then, as the product was still fairly new; I'm not sure it even had a "jobs" section back then. I wasn't "independent" for very long before my old boss, Bob, reached out to me inquiring about my situation. It seemed as if he had been on a similar path, and somehow ended up contracting with an ecommerce company in Chicago.

At the time, I hadn't even formed an LLC, but that didn't deter me from discussing the opportunity with Bob. This was my first real "contracting/consulting" discussion, and I was interviewed by a few people Bob put me in touch with from this Chicago based company. This went well, and I remember having conversations with my wife about the things I was scared most of, mainly the travel every week and how it would affect our home life. At least the travel was just to one city, Chicago, so it would be easy to get to.

As luck would have it, my father-in-law turned out to be available to help with the kids—at this point, I was now up to two, adding my lovely daughter Nora to the mix—and this was very good, as it would form a great bond between him and the kids that I'm sure he and they still value enormously. There was of course some lingering consternation on the decision, but it was a great opportunity; and, hey, someone was going to teach me about a profession, industry, and technology I'd never had exposure to, which was exciting.

Then came the conversation about payment: I could hardly believe what they were going to pay me per hour just to "learn." I think my wife felt the same, so the discussion was short: for that amount of money, we could make it happen. End of discussion. I was still caught up in how much money I was making and the "default path" to get a better life, and I didn't really take into account hours worked, or travel, or other quality-of-life concepts that came to me much later in my career.

🗝 Chapter Takeaways: Your Reputation Matters More Than Your Next Paycheck

1. When The Values Don't Match, You Can't Unsee It
   From fast-paced agency life to the for-profit education engine, I began to recognize the gap between my values and the product we worked on. Once I saw this, staying wasn't an option—even without a next step lined up.

2. Digital Was Becoming Strategy—And I Was Learning Fast
   I was executing campaigns, but I was also learning A/B testing, building websites and translating between stakeholders. It wasn't always cool or glamorous, but it was foundational. I was becoming a strategist.

3. "Just Make Sure It Doesn't Suck" Is A Philosophy
   It seemed like a throwaway comment, but there *was* something to be learned from this. Don't let perfect get in the way

of good enough. You have to pick your battles, and sometimes you have to move forward no matter what to hit the bigger goal. I'd carry that mindset into higher-stakes work later.

4. Quitting Without A Plan Can Be the Right Move—If It Comes From Integrity
Walking away with nothing lined up isn't reckless if it's done to reclaim self-respect. When I rejected the for-profit education job, I rejected a system I no longer believed in. Maybe it takes guts, but it also takes self-trust.

5. A Pivot Starts With One Connection—And A Click
Updating LinkedIn, getting a message from Bob, and saying yes to a contract. That's how reinvention begins. I wasn't fully clear on what was next, but I was willing, and the path met me halfway.

CHAPTER 5

2010: How Saying Yes Before You're Ready Can Accelerate Your Career by Years

eCommerce: Not Knowing Something Is An Opportunity

After accepting the position after being independent for only a few weeks—ah, the golden days, when it was so much easier then to get work than it has been over the past several years!—I wasted no time trying to get up to speed on everything.

During the interview process, two things stuck out.

First: had I ever heard of this technology called "eCommerce"?

Second: had I ever heard of a certain large MRO company?

The answer was no to both, but clearly they were eager to get bodies in the door, as I was accepted pretty rapidly. It probably also helped to have Bob in my corner: remember kids, a lot of success comes down to networking and "who you know", so get out there and schmooze! There were also ideas and buzzwords thrown around like "business analyst," "waterfall," "agile," "Water-Scrum-Fall," Hybris (some small upstart eComm company out of Germany later bought by SAP), IDEO, SAP ERP, UX, front end, back end, PMI, and so on. Some of this was familiar to me, but most of it wasn't. Clearly, I had a lot to learn.

Your Baseline For "Good Work" Gets Set Early—Make Sure It's High

I was very fortunate to join this project at a time when this certain large MRO company was kicking off a major transformation in its business. They had just gone through a large SAP ERP transformation, and now it was time to move toward eCommerce. In a funny twist of fate and luck, it was a scion of management consulting, one of the MBB firms and the same one I worked with at Wharton and would later be entwined with, that had made this recommendation.

The weaving of this company in and out of my life is very prescient. When I first started, it was so early for the company that we were still huddling in a windowless room in Lake Forest at the large MRO company's HQ. This was something all too familiar to my consultant brethren that would repeat itself numerous times throughout my career—bonus if you got a room with a window. We had the opportunity to be there for a major launch celebration that featured a skit with employees dressed as cheerleaders, as well as the unveiling of the work (and probably lots of money for said work) done for the MRO company by a world-famous design and consulting firm from California. To be fair, it was good work, and something that would leave a lasting impression on me on how a digital transformation "should be done."

Admittedly, the bar was set very high. What do I mean by this? The biggest common mistake these companies make when embarking on these transformations is that they don't really get to know their customers, or the "persona" of their customers. A lot of times the executives think they know what the customer wants or what is best for them—but often, of course, they are wrong. The California-based design and consulting firm unveiled to us the top personas that engaged with the large MRO company, by putting sample faces, names, backgrounds, functions they do with the MRO company, pain points, needs, etc.

The California firm's approach taught me what I now call the "Persona-First Transformation" method—a framework I've used many times, which may have even more importance for AI implementations.

It went down at the large MRO company like this:

Discovery Phase: Who are your actual users? Instead of assuming, the California-based design and consulting firm went into the field, shadowing maintenance workers, procurement managers, and small business owners. They found that the "customer" was often more of an ecosystem instead of a single person: the people searching, approving, and using the products might all be different.

Definition Phase: What do they really need? Not what executives thought they needed, but what the personas actually struggled with. The hypothetical maintenance supervisor didn't need to sift through 50,000 SKUs online—what he really needed might be more like reordering his standard supplies in under 30 seconds between emergencies.

Design Phase: How do we serve those needs? This is where requirements needed to meet whatever the reality was. Every feature had to map back to a specific persona's specific need. If there was no persona, there was no feature. This kept us from building what I call "executive vanity features"—things that demo well in boardrooms but fail on the ground.

Delivery Phase: How do we roll out without breaking trust? We launched first to the smaller persona groups that had fewer complexities, so we weren't disrupting the larger groups in the beginning or those that we knew were more complex. This allowed us to work the kinks out and not take down huge parts of the business or crash the technology.

Every argument and decision came back to a question like: "What would Mike the Maintenance Manager do with this?" This insistence on starting with users rather than technology is why our large MRO company transformation succeeded where so many others had failed.

Yes, the bar was set *very* high for me on my first digital consulting engagement. The work was so good we made sure to take the large boards with all that information on them of the different personas and put them all over the walls where we worked downtown.

"Downtown," you ask? "I thought you were in Lake Forest," you astutely recall. Great memory! But that was only a short time. In a move to "unify" the team more and keep them away from distractions, the decision was made to take the Chicago ecommerce company's consultants, the Hybris developers, and those other independent consultants and hand-picked large MRO company employees and co-locate them downtown in Chicago at the Ogilvie train station building. I was new to this, and it was confusing to me. Why have us sequestered away from the client and not onsite with them in Lake Forest? I'm sure others have better insights than I do on this move, but it would be repeated another time for me later, when I worked for a very large quick-serve restaurant chain from the Chicago area…

Chicago Every Week—The Life of a Traveling Consultant

The People You Travel With Become Some Of Your Closest Colleagues

Well, at first I was a bit bummed about not being onsite with the client, but I quickly realized that being in downtown Chicago had way more to offer than sleepy Lake Forest after (and before) work. There was only a small amount of us traveling in every week from out of town, and it was me, Bob and someone else Bob had hired and worked with in the past, Simon. All the consultants that may be reading this know what that meant: *lots* of personal time with Bob and Simon for me in my future. Which wasn't a bad thing! Another very good thing for me was that Bob and Simon were big time runners and loved to workout. I couldn't keep up with them on the running but still it pushed me to get out there and run every day after work, along with taking advantage of the amazing hotel gym we had, which was bigger than most *regular* gyms.

Where would one find such an amazing gym in downtown Chicago at a hotel? Well, it would be the world-famous Palmer House Hotel. For those that don't know, the Palmer House has amazing history in the Chicago area. It was one of the only structures not to burn down during the Great Chicago Fire of 1871. It is a historical landmark, and even hosted the likes of Capone back in the day. There are ghost tours; the architecture and old-world ambience it displays to me are second to none. It wasn't the fanciest of places, but I really loved the architecture and feel. It was a long way from the "regular" management consultant hotels like the Ritz and Four Seasons, and me, Bob and Simon made this home for well over a year. It's a hotel I would come back to many times for work and family trips.

By the end of almost a year on the project, I was third on the list for most nights slept at the Palmer House. This irritated Bob, but he was an executive and had to travel to other places while I was just a lowly BA that was happy to have consistency in travel and be soaking up all the great education that had been coming my way.

Showing Up Early And Staying Curious Compounds Into Expertise

I tended to be an early riser compared to my peers, so I was in the office before a lot of people—I was the first one in many times. It helped that I was from the East Coast and had an hour more than them to adjust. One of the side benefits of this was a lot more time with the few other people that would get to the office early, mainly my boss Dave and our User Experience lead, Jeff. This led to a lot of good morning banter over coffee, but also taught me a lot. A lot of people like to focus on "the grind" and how many hours you put into the work, and there's admittedly a lot to be argued about that nowadays—but pre-Covid, that perception was pretty heavy. To me, it meant building rapport with my boss Dave and building relationships with someone like Jeff, who was from a totally different department, skillset, and background than me. It helped me when Jeff took me under his wing to teach me about things like promotions, cross-selling and upselling—and, most importantly, user experience, and how important it was in the digital world.

The Power Of Personas, Customer Experience, And Heuristic Analysis

This is an age-old tech debate: should you build to meet your requirements before you build the user experience (UX) or User Interface (UI)? Or should you build the UX/UI first, and *then* fill in with the requirements?

And to break down the requirements even further: are they functional or technical requirements?

My answer, which seems to be shared by a lot of people I've talked to, is neither. You have to have a clear vision in place before getting into tech and architecture or user experience. The large MRO company did this through their work with the major MBB firm I'd later work at, first laying out and weighing the costs and the benefits of doing this large digital transformation. Then they took a next step in clearly defining why they were doing this, and who they were doing it for, through their work with the California-based design and consulting firm.

The next step from that is execution, and to our sales team's credit, they won the deal. I know Bob and Mike, who both interviewed and hired me for this, were heavily involved. Apparently we had been doing work there for a while, and through "right place, right time" and a hell of a sales job, the Chicago ecommerce company beat out another large consulting firm, as well as perhaps several other companies, and landed a massive deal for the small company that would put it on the map, as well as in the eventual crosshairs of acquisition for said large consulting firm.

But I digress. The work of the California firm and then Jeff and his team to incorporate the personas, heuristic analysis, and UX throughout a very functional and technical process was amazing, and something I never really saw repeated on a big transformation like that again. The co-location in downtown Chicago did help, as well, and the walls and walls of print-outs on the latest changes and required functions that were mapped out (and changed daily) helped foster collaborative conversations. You could easily pull in the functional BAs like me and the technical people (the developers and architects) to have a robust discussion with the designers to make sure everyone was on the same page, which also helped. Finally, all of this was done while being managed by the project management and leadership layers to make sure we were hitting our goals and checking the boxes. I found it all quite impressive.

Writing Requirements That I Now See as Standard/ Table Stakes In The eCommerce Package We Were Working With (Yeah, I'm Old)

A big part of our BA job was running workshops to elicit functional (and some technical) requirements with the large MRO company executives to help us build out what would become one of the largest B2B2C websites ever, especially the largest on Hybris, which, again, was a German software platform operating in North America. There were several of us BAs working for Dave, and we did a good job, though he would probably jokingly say we didn't, of organizing along the different steps in the customer journey to help break up and organize the requirements. This meant having the workshops, then a series of sleuthing missions with the architects, developers and UI/UX people to see what was actually feasible. Then once that was determined, seeing what would be standard, or what we call "out of the box" from Hybris, that could help accomplish this, or what would have to be "custom" that the large MRO company would have to pay for to accomplish these requirements.

If it was decided that custom work was needed, then there was a discussion with the business on whether it was *really* needed for the extra cost. If it was, then we needed to have the business unit justify it with a business case, and then finally help rank all these custom and out-of-the-box things they wanted.

The project management teams and leadership from the large MRO company and the Chicago ecommerce company did a great job at turning this back onto the business to make sure all these things were needed. It was collaborative, indeed, but there were also some tough discussions. A lot of these requirements ended up at least being "slightly" custom, which I look back on now and find it ironic that I helped write some of these requirements that eventually Hybris would take and turn into standard out-of-the-box requirements for their software eCommerce package. I remember being surprised later when in meetings with clients, as we talked through requirements and assessed and compared eCommerce packages, finding out that SAP (the company that would later buy Hybris) had incorporated them as standard out-of-the-box things. It was always cool to see that, though it probably dated me when I would yell, "I wrote that requirement!"

It's wild to think about those late nights writing requirements that would eventually become industry standard. Now I'm watching the same thing happen with AI implementations, where today's custom ChatGPT integration is tomorrow's baseline expectation. The pattern is identical: early adopters pay premium prices to figure it out, then whatever it is they figure out becomes table stakes. If you're implementing AI today, you're essentially writing the playbook everyone else will follow down the road.

Discovering What eCommerce Was and Could Do

I don't think it fully dawned on me the power of eCommerce at the time, especially with it not being that mature yet. Sure, I was helping "enroll" people for the for-profit college system as part of my job, but we weren't doing the transactions online: someone had to call them to seal the deal on that front. So this whole world of taking actual payments online was very new to me, and it meant there were a lot more rules and things to be mindful of when it came to payments. Things like privacy, transaction times, payment to vendors, promotion tie-ins to pricing, checkout, cart, and so on.

This was also in the days before the EU's General Data Protection Regulation (GDPR), big data leaks, and all the rules that would come out later to help secure these transactions. This was going to require a big mindshift not only with the large MRO company's customers but their sales people. They were all used to the "big red book" sales process that required sales people to go out (or be present in a physical store for when a customer came in) to take the orders, then manually enter them in somewhere and both make sure that the customer got the items and that the large MRO got paid. Do you know how many steps in the process this eCommerce thing was going to help eliminate on that front? It was rapid change, and huge mindshift, for sure. I remember there being a lot of discussion and pushback from sales to make sure that they would get correct attribution and commission for their sales in this new digital platform—lots of meetings were spent making sure this would happen. Then there was eventually a rollout of iPads to help replace the big red books, and much change and training came along with that to help teach the sales people how to use them, enter orders and make sure they got their commission. This was done on a very large scale, and there were so many things that could have gone wrong. Though I'm certain some did, pulling this huge effort off at the time was, in the end, very successful.

The Power of Promotions

Percentages Off, Dollars Off, Free Shipping, Free Item, Combination: "Jamie, It's That Simple."

My buddy Jeff, mentioned earlier as part of the early morning crew, took me under his wing when I had a workshop coming up at the beginning to gather requirements about promotions, and how they should be executed from an eCommerce perspective. I was very new, so I was eager to take his advice and get the coaching. Jeff could take complex things and break them down in a very simple way, which I attribute to his user experience background.

One day, we gathered in a room and he outlined to me the five different high-level ways that one could derive a promotion—as mentioned in the title of this chapter—drew them up in a simple five-circle explanation, and that was it. It seemed so simple at the time, but the visual was so powerful that I made sure to turn it into part of a PowerPoint. I'd ultimately use that slide for many years after; it had special relevance for all the other consulting firms I'd work at later, as it stayed very relevant.

It was a huge lesson for me: in digital commerce, complexity can kill adoption. You can design the most sophisticated promotions engine in the world, but if your customer can't understand it, it's not helping anyone.

I adapted what Jeff showed me into what I call a "Promotions and Simplicity Model." It rests on a single principle: if you can't explain it in five levers or fewer, it doesn't scale.

The Five Levers of Digital Promotion:

1. **Discounts**—Percent-off, dollar-off, or buy-one-get-one.
2. **Free Shipping/Delivery**—Still one of the most powerful incentives.
3. **Loyalty Rewards**—Earn-and-use points or credits.
4. **Bundling**—Encourage higher average order value through packaged offers.
5. **Seasonal/Scarcity Triggers**—Limited time, exclusive access, or seasonal relevance.

Everything else tends to be a variation on these five. If your team is inventing the sixth or seventh lever, stop and ask if you're just making things more complicated than they have to be. The most successful digital programs I've seen were built to be simple.

On a personal note, I kept in touch with Jeff for many years after when I would return to Chicago. It was always great getting back together with him and some of the old crew from the large MRO company: we really did share a whole year (and more) together every single day in close quarters. We went to battle together and were always there to support each other. Just recently, though, I thought of him again and made a post about him on LinkedIn, only to learn from a former colleague that Jeff had sadly passed away. I was, of course, sad and shocked to hear it; he had always been so full of life, and I really owed him a lot for my career trajectory. Rest in Peace, Jeff.

The Early Days of "Loyalty" And What That Meant At The Time

Not only did the rise of "loyalty" entail questions about how to capture these large MRO company customers online or digitally to get and create more loyalty from them, but there was also a whole change of how you got very long-term and loyal customers of the large MRO company that were tied to a certain expectation and way of working with that company to accept new methods. Their expectations had been to go through a sales rep, use a big red book, or call or visit a store, but now, there was the entirely new channel of "digital" to get educated on and accustomed to, on top of smartphones and what could be done with an iPad. It was a big risk to take this all on—a big change and big transformation in general—so I give the leadership team at the large MRO company a gigantic amount of credit for realizing they needed to change. It was going to be painful, but it needed to happen. These promotions were a way to help foster more loyalty, and as I will break down in the next chapter, not all promotions were created equal, as they differed by customer across business-to-business and business-to-customer.

Business-To-Business, Business-To-Customer, And Business-To-Business-To-Customer: Know The Difference, And What That Entails

Complexity Of Requirements

Not only was I learning all these new skills, in a totally newer industry for me, but then it was also that I had to learn what was required to make this eCommerce transformation work in the business-to-business (B2B), business-to-consumer (B2C), and the certain instances of B2B customers that could also then purchase items on a B2C journey termed B2B2C. For this, it helps to think of a janitor who purchases material for the school he works at, but may have a hobby or side business fixing up old houses, and wants to purchase things from a large MRO company for himself. Not only were we dealing with this layer, creating great and complex B2B experiences while also keeping in mind what the B2C persona would need, but there were complex layers with the B2B customers. The large MRO company had categories for government, education, and so on of personas defined, and not all of them had, wanted, or needed the same experiences, so there could be slight nuances. When you then add in the tiers of permissions and super users that were experiencing the MRO company's website, you could easily see why our requirements lists were well in the thousands (or even tens of thousands) of requirements!

The Threat Of Amazon

I would be remiss not to mention another factor in why the large MRO company felt the urgency to start this transformation (besides its work with the large MBB firm and market forces): Amazon. They were rumored to be starting a large B2B MRO-like experience themselves to eventually rival their efforts in the area of B2C. This was putting the large MRO company and its competitors on high alert, but reflecting on it now, it was the kick in the pants those companies needed to "digitize" themselves and start these massive transformations.

🔑 Chapter Takeaways: From Digital Rookie To eComm Architect

1. Saying "Yes" Even Before You're Ready Can Still Lead To Greatness
   I didn't know what eCommerce was, and at first I hadn't heard of the certain large MRO company. But I said yes, leaned in, and learned fast. That single move unlocked an entire new career path for me. It was extremely important.

2. Mentorship + Proximity = Growth At Warp Speed
   Between morning coffee talks with Jeff and Dave, consistent time with Bob and Simon, and absorbing UX best practices from the project led by the California-based design and consulting firm, I was doing more than learning—I was accelerating.

3. Strategy Must Start With The Customer, Not The Tech
   Personas, pain points, and user journeys were our foundation. I saw first-hand how human-centered strategy, when you do it right, creates focus and unity across massive digital efforts.

4. What You Build Today Can Become The Industry Standard Tomorrow
   The requirements I helped define became part of the core feature set in SAP's eCommerce suite. That's legacy work—and a reminder that details matter, even, or especially, when no one's watching.

5. Transformation Is Personal Before It's Organizational
   It wasn't just the large MRO company that had to evolve—their sales teams, their customers, and their culture all had to chang too. Watching that shift taught me that digital work is human work, first and foremost.

6. Promotions Are Simple Until They Aren't
   What seems like "$10 off" on the surface opens up a world of UX, tech, and strategy decisions. Jeff's five-promo model became a teaching tool that grounded my approach for years.

7. My Curiosity Compounded Into Career Capital
   I entered as a curious outsider, and left the project as someone fluent in B2B, B2C, and B2B2C complexity—with scars, successes, and a clear sense of what it means to lead digital transformation.

Bonus Takeaways:

The persona-emphasizing approach we did with the large MRO company provides a great framework for other projects, so I've broken it down here:

Persona-First Approach:

1. **Discovery:** Study real users in their actual environment
2. **Definition:** Document specific needs by persona type
3. **Design:** Build only what serves identified persona needs
4. **Delivery:** Roll out by persona readiness, not arbitrary timelines

Implications for AI? Companies these days want to build and use AI products for "everyone" instead of asking: Who specifically will use this? A customer service rep needs different AI tools than a financial analyst. Without personas, you have AI tools at high cost that just sit there and gather digital dust.

How Past Experience Applies To Current and Oncoming Challenges with AI

- **In the past, with large MRO company:** Sales teams feared eCommerce would eliminate commissions.
- **Now, with AI:** Employees fear AI will eliminate jobs.
- **The insight:** "Success requires bringing existing teams along as enablers, not replacing them wholesale"

CHAPTER 6

Why the "Perfect Opportunity" Can Be a Dead End— And How to Spot It Early

Thanks For Coming On Board! Now See You Later!

It's funny how early experiences can really shape where you go and how you get there later in your career. I'm simply going to call this firm an "ICF" (Indian Consulting Firm) which was one of many at the time trying to spin up "management consulting" groups in the US and pull in various talent from the likes of Deloitte, Accenture, and so on.

Somehow, they recruited me at the time, and seeing Accenture on the horizon as potentially acquiring the Chicago ecommerce company, I wanted to explore my options. The people I met at the time that were heading this group in the US were smart and had great experience. I was eager to start a new chapter and learn new skills, but also take what I had learned over the past three years and "test the market."

It only lasted about 11 months.

Unfortunately, those who had interviewed me and whom I worked for quickly started peeling off once the shine started to wear off against the jump in pay. There were a *lot* of internal policies (mailing receipts to India for reimbursement, *maybe* 6-8 weeks later) that just made doing business impossible. Over time all the red tape wears on you and frustration sets in: it quickly did so for me and many others.

"You Don't Know What You're Talking About"—The Constant Questioning of Expertise

One of my longest and best projects during that time was for an education B2B and B2C company that was going to implement eCommerce. They, too, needed to tackle the B2B and B2C challenges like the large MRO company had.

It lasted several months, and there were many ups and downs. I do remember it was in the Chicago suburb of Oak Brook—a place you'll see I would be coming back to years down the road—and when we were there it was almost the coldest I can remember ever being in Chicago. It was one of those winters where you get the rental car going, have the heat on full blast, and you're *still* freezing by the time you get back to the hotel twenty minutes later. I was confident and could handle myself well enough at the client site, but what really started to wear me down was the constant questioning by my colleagues on my expertise, skills and strategies. I understand a little as to why, since I was new to them and it was intense at times with the client, and I'm also sure they realized that this offshore-predominant model wasn't landing well with this client. It also didn't help that I was one of the only non-Indians from the firm on the project. Racial concerns or no, the result of this was that a good deal of the Midwestern, white clientele came to me a lot.

So there was trouble on both sides, you could say. Some great work did come out of this project, though, including working side-by-side with a person that would play a very large role in helping me out on a big opportunity at my next port of call. There'll be more to come on that later.

"Jamie, Don't Ever Cancel A Vacation For This Job": Words Of Wisdom

This is a brief story, but I'll always remember and be grateful for someone I worked with and respected very much at this company. His name was Ken. We were both working on a big proposal for a potential client (a railroad client: my first and only ever) and this required a lot of late-night calls with India offshore to help move the proposal forward while also working during the day. It was forcing us to work very long hours.

I had a vacation coming up that we were really looking forward to, but me not being at this company that long and wanting to impress/improve while there had me thinking of cancelling it. Ken had been and would continue to be very successful, but before he'd gotten into his current position, he'd actually happened to have played football from Notre Dame—and the football-like coaching he gave me at this moment has stuck with me ever since. He told me to never, ever cancel a vacation for a job, but especially *this* job. I know he was talking about this specific one, at least partly probably because I'd seen him weather some serious heat from the executives, which I always credited him for, but I used that advice to make sure I remembered and honored him in that moment and then beyond to guard against ever considering doing something like that again. I've tried to pass this advice down to others ever since. No job is worth canceling a vacation for a multitude of reasons, which I'll soon be getting to. Oddly enough, later on during my time at the MBB firm, I would start hearing this offered in roundtable review discussions of our employees as a sign that they were taking the job more seriously. I eventually realized I was hearing this more and more, which made me in turn more and more *alarmed* as I noticed my values beginning to drift from the company's. I started to see that my days were numbered...

Where Did All The People Go Who Just Hired Me!?

As mentioned, people started to leave the company soon after I joined; their grand vision just didn't seem to be working out. First my boss left, then their boss. It was like dominos falling, and a race to the exit. I quickly started my networking in earnest, and before long made a connection to a consulting firm based out of France but growing in North America (and with the intent to expand even more). This turned into a great career move, and one that really helped propel my stock in the digital world. But as with moving to Knowledge@ Wharton early in my career, it would take a measure of believing the vision and acting on the entrepreneurial opportunity in front of me.

🔑 Chapter Takeaways: The Wrong Fit Can Sometimes Still Move You Forward

1. Sometimes The Vision Looks Right Until You're Inside It
   Big names, smart people, and a good pitch pulled me in, but beneath the polish, I found red tape, high turnover, and systems that slowed me down instead of setting me up.

2. Proximity Doesn't Equal Alignment
   I was on the front lines with the ICF, but they were questioning me behind the scenes. This was a problem with trust, style, and culture, and when that's off, the work gets heavier than it needs to be.

3. "Don't Cancel That Vacation" Is Career Advice Disguised as Life Wisdom
   Ken's words were about time off, sure, but they were also about boundaries, respect, and remembering who you are outside a job. That mindset became a guardrail for me for years to come.

4. The Ones Who Hire You Might Not Stay to Help You
   Watching leadership peel off, one by one, taught me to spot
   instability sooner. Loyalty has limits when the ship is sinking,
   and sometimes the best move is just to get out with your head
   held high.

5. Even A Wrong Turn Can Point You Somewhere Better
   This chapter ended with a new connection, a new opportunity, and the start of something far more aligned with what I
   wanted and needed. The next leap from a bad situation can be
   huge in a great way, even if it might not be perfect.

CHAPTER 7

The Art of Speaking Truth to Power Without Losing Your Job (And Sometimes Winning Big)

Getting To Atlanta During An Ice Storm

I was all set to have interviews in Atlanta, in the upscale Buckhead neighborhood, when a day before my flight the city was hit by one of the largest ice storms ever seen in the American Southeast. It's funny how I remember some of these important times in my life by the weather at the time—like when I was at the large MRO company and a snowstorm in Chicago locked us inside the Palmer House for two days while Lake Shore Drive was shut down. In the case of Atlanta, this ice storm wreaked havoc across the city, with people having to abandon their cars on the highways and walk to work, so my interviews were delayed a bit.

White Board Session With The North America Head

The French consulting firm's head of North America at the time had started and grown his career at a company it later acquired. He was a no-nonsense person and leader, and could connect with people and break down stories as well as big challenges to keep them relatable.

The narrative he used to sell me on the firm was this: he walked up to a whiteboard in his room and started charting out where it stood against the likes of Deloitte and Accenture when it came to digital transformation and eCommerce opportunities/wins. It wasn't good, to put it mildly, and I may even remember him saying "Jamie, we're getting our asses kicked by these guys." Because of this, he was starting a small team in North America to try to catch up and was wondering if I wanted to join. It probably wasn't the hardest negotiation they'd ever had, as the situation I was coming out of was *much* worse. In the end, it was a great decision, and one that would set me up for success and lead to many opportunities down the road.

Tales From The Road:

Atlanta And The Building Of A Team

After I joined our "big" group of five or six people in "digital transformation," I was quickly staffed on a project in Atlanta, again in the Buckhead neighborhood. We did a quick three-month engagement to help their team with user experience work. The client was very nice but very busy, a trend all of us consultants know too well, so it was hard to get a lot of guidance from them when working through our solutions. I do remember being thankful for the experience at the Chicago ecommerce company, as it helped me relate and manage our various resources in different areas like customer experience and technical needs. I was becoming more confident in my skills and abilities, and the past experiences helped me to be prepared for that. From an organizational standpoint, my boss (not the head of North America but the person in between us) would only be there a short time; this would start the trend of my several years at the French consulting firm of having an unusually large number of bosses. But as

I was learning in consulting, bosses were not bosses in the traditional sense. It was the "matrix" lesson I was beginning to learn in this field. My boss was really only there to help guide me, gather feedback from others I was working with, then grade me at the end of the year based on the feedback he had gathered.

The Dallas-Based QSR Story

Be Humble And Just Put The Product Details Into The Spreadsheet (How Many Calories In That?)

So as things were winding up at the French firm, we happened to get into an engagement with a Dallas-based QSR to help them with strategy and eventual execution in setting up their online website for ordering for pickup—this being before delivery options via apps had become so prevalent. The catch was that there had been a small team from the French firm already working for them, so I was being brought in to see if we could get them to agree to a larger deal and longer engagement. One of my peers, Mark, was pretty much already leading the account and was local, which was great, so I realized that the normal stuff I would do to "lead" the account really wasn't needed. So I looked for where I could add value, didn't get hung up on what exact "role" I would be playing, and did what I needed to do to help support the team and grow the account. I ended up doing a lot of running around the Dallas QSR company getting product details to then input into a spreadsheet that would be uploaded into the eCommerce engine. I could have easily whined and complained about it and told the French firm they were wasting my talents, but I realized that A) this was a great way to learn more about the products; B) This was a great way to meet a lot of different people at the client, and C) This was a great way to help the team out as best as I could without getting in the way. One of the most memorable things doing this was learning about all the nutritional and caloric values of these foods. Huge amounts of calories and sodium for the most trivial foods. I decided to stick with the salmon a lot when eating there. In any case, I would never have never thought this would be the beginning of a career with so many quick-serve restaurant (QSR) opportunities in my life.

From A Boss At The French Firm: "Failure Is Not An Option, Sorry, Our Flight Leaves In An Hour."

We had a very smart and confident boss at the time who'd been successful at his previous company and was leading our group. Lately he'd been constantly flying to places to get our group business, and I'm sure it wasn't an easy job. As we were about to pitch a multi-million dollar opportunity, he and our sales person visited us at the client site in Dallas, met the client, then took me and the other leader to the side for a sort of briefing. We had a very deep technical person who knew the platform we were going to help install at the Dallas-based QSR, and he knew the client well, but the issue was that he was a bit "sensitive" when it came to feedback—especially when the client or teammates pushed back on what he was proposing. Our boss didn't mince words, and told us we needed to figure out how to manage this very aloof person and get him to comply more, especially as this pitch was about to happen. He emphasized that we needed not to screw it up; his exact words were that "failure is not an option."

It felt bad to get a message like this from our boss, though, the man technically leading our group. He was asking us to manage our colleague and his quirks, but it was *his* job to do this, not ours. On top of any managerial title, he was literally the VP. This would be the first of many times I worked with people with personality needs that had to be considered, understood, and accommodated to the best of my ability. It wasn't easy, to be sure.

Our Expert In eCommerce Just Walked Out

This project had many ups and downs. As we were gearing up for this big pitch to the CIO to secure the next big phase, the sensitive savant we were supposed to accommodate decided to be extra-sensitive and caused some drama with the client. He walked out of their building abruptly, doing it in such a way that we had no idea if he'd come back or not. The trouble was, we had to prepare our pitch with a CIO at the Dallas QSR who had a connection with the savant, and it would look very bad for us if he wasn't there. We finished the presentation preparations on our own, not knowing what would happen, but the savant returned at just the right moment to answer the hard technical questions. Later, I worked on a larger project with him where he really impressed me with his technical skill. He knew what he was doing, and ran fantastic workshops—but God help you if you accidentally stepped on his toes. It was either love or hate between him, and you, and a client.

Sick As A Dog, Can Barely Talk, But I Need To Make The Big Pitch!

A few days before the pitch, I got very sick. I could barely make it out of bed to get to the prep sessions, and it was touch-and-go for the whole preparatory period. I somehow rallied with lots of medications, thanked god I didn't have too much of a speaking role, and got my ass into the client office to make the pitch. I was *extremely* glad this teammate of mine had made it back in for the pitch: it gave me the chance to just sit in the back and sweat profusely. I could barely talk, but apparently everything still looked good for the client, and we sealed the deal. This was the beginning of a year-long effort to bring eCommerce to the Dallas-based QSR, and one of the first big deals I helped win. It would give me immense satisfaction, to be sure, as well as give me the desire to do this kind of thing even more.

Jamie Breaks Out In Hives: "I Swear It's Not Gonorrhea..."

Being one of the leaders on the Dallas QSR project meant I was going to Dallas every week. It was a lot of good work, but also a lot of stress—not only on the business side, but also on the personal side. I was grateful that my then-father-in-law could help out with the kids, but it also meant I wasn't home to connect more with the family.

This period was the first time stress caused me to break out in hives all over my body. I had never had this before; it was very strange. Not knowing what was going on, I went to a clinic and waited with some very questionable people in a questionable neighborhood in Dallas to be seen by someone. They had to take samples, and the doctor thought it might be gonorrhea. This was shocking to me: where could I have possibly gotten *gonorrhea*? I told my wife at the time, just to be up-front about the possibility, but guaranteed her I hadn't gone to any strip clubs or brothels in Dallas when I went there every week.

Fortunately the test results came back negative, which helped confirm the stress-caused diagnosis. I was just *extremely* stressed. It was awful, and I would happen to experience this a second time several years later. Around the time I was divorced, I took the kids to San Diego for a trip and, despite having a great time with them, woke up in the hotel in downtown in a sweat and completely breaking out in hives. Again, it was stress related.

It's scary to think how much you bury or brush off that can subconsciously stack up inside of you until it surfaces in ailments or breaks down your body. I had to leave the kids alone in the middle of the night, run to CVS to get some Benadryl and quickly run back.

I was better by the morning, but this clearly sent a message to me. Stress-induced hives was a symptom of oncoming burnout, and apparently I had a habit of ignoring the warning signs—the tight chest, the Sunday night dread, failing to laugh at funny things; all of that. Your body knows what's going on, even when you're pretending everything's fine. If you're reading this and recognizing yourself in any of it, don't do what I did—don't wait for full-blown burnout to admit something's wrong.

So after the first hives incident I started to try, at least, to meditate. I would try to focus each morning or night at the crappy Hampton Inn in Dallas we were staying at near the client—with very loud noises outside from the street constantly interrupting my concentration. It was hard for me then, and it's hard for me now; I've never found meditation easy, and I don't practice it daily, like some people recommend. But I do try to make it part of my routine when I can.

The "Bay Area Beauty Brand" Story

Multi-Level Marketing (MLM) And The Implications Of Digital

After things started winding down at the Dallas-based QSR, I found myself called to San Francisco to help sell a company that had a fascinating background. I really hadn't paid much attention to the multi-level marketing space since my days in college when I was exposed to Amway (Google it, kids) and found it a bit disturbing how it relied so heavily on family and friends to help peddle your products. But suddenly, here I was at the company headquarters in downtown San Francisco working with someone recently brought in to head their digital work. The company was a bit unusual for having a product created by two Ivy League researcher-doctors (which granted, of course, instant credibility) and also being high-end, which meant a higher price point. The key thing they were missing was being able to sell online.

Big Bang Vs. Rollout By User Group: "Jamie You Are A Dinosaur"

As part of this eCommerce re-platforming project, we came to learn that the IT leadership team wanted to do a "big bang" rollout of the platform. What does that mean? It means you do exactly the opposite of the large MRO company (and many other successful companies), where you choose to flip everyone over to a new plat-form on Day One rather than breaking up the user groups and rolling out to them one group at a time. The advantage of doing that is that it gives you the chance to course-correct or handle issues as they come up with smaller groups rather than everyone, all at once, which can be huge mess—and in extreme cases, you end up rolling back to the original site, which should be avoided at all costs. It's like admitting defeat.

Well, I was brought in to meet with the lead IT person on the project, who reported to the CIO. When I discovered from him that he had planned to do this Big Bang approach, I couldn't help myself from advising against it. I told him that going Big Bang would be a mistake, which he wasn't happy to hear. He also didn't like my suggestion of following the large MRO company approach, which clearly went against his plans. Right in front of his direct reports he called me a "dinosaur" and said Big Bang was the way to go. Not wanting to lose the contract for the French firm, and keep our team in place, I acquiesced—but deep down, as you might imagine, I knew this wasn't going to end well.

As it happened, I wouldn't be working with them when they even-tually launched, but they stuck to Big Bang and it was, of course, a disaster, losing millions of dollars and forcing them to roll back the site. I didn't celebrate when I heard about this, but I *did* forward some of my original communications warning against Big Bang to a few colleagues. You know: for future reference.

By the time this occurred, the French firm was only running the change management piece, as they had given responsibility for eCommerce execution to another firm. I felt vindicated, to say the least. The IT leaders responsible for that mess were scattered to the wind after that.

Speaking Up Based On Your Experiences And The Ramifications It Can Have In Your Work Life

The valuable lesson this taught me was that those that try to act like they're the smartest in the room usually aren't. There was little-to-no consensus-building with this person and their team: no openness to other ideas, humbleness, crowdsourcing ideas, or anything like that. At least I felt that at this point in my career, I had enough experience to offer my viewpoints. If people didn't want to listen, then it was on them. Sometimes we feel like we need to keep quiet when it comes to our experiences, but we need to share them.

You never know when they could help—sometimes to a gigantic extent. My recommended phased approach would have cost a tiny fraction of the millions of dollars the company ultimately lost, and that's to say nothing of the brand damage.

I now use this as a teaching case with some of my clients. If someone calls your experience-based concerns "outdated," that might be one of the times they need that experience most.

The Best Boss/Mentor I Ever Had; The Signs Of Good Emotional Intelligence

My boss during this project was Pete. He was great, taught me a lot, and really cared for me and our team. His emotional intelligence and thoughtfulness were a breath of fresh air in the consulting area, as typical bosses there didn't tend to care too much about their teams or employees. The standard attitude was to win at all costs, burn the midnight oil, and deliver that value, or else.

I was shocked by how much time and thought Pete eventually put into my employee review at the French firm. My bosses would normally just add one or two lines and that would be it—and later, at the large MBB firm I worked at, my bosses would focus the majority of feedback just on "areas for improvement." Pete was a great role model at the time, and I took his "lead by example" to heart when dealing with people I had to provide reviews for.

Traveling To San Francisco For Nine Months Straight

Throughout my career I had been very fortunate to be on consulting engagements in cities that were easy to get to without much travel time. Chicago, Philadelphia, New York, even Dallas. These were all a direct flight from Pittsburgh. But the San Francisco project was a big deal, and I was a key component, so I needed to stay on it. This meant a lot of flights back and forth, which also meant connections and red-eyes sometimes. Not the best. By the time I would acclimate to Pacific Time during the week, it would be time for me to get on a plane and go home. For a while, I was the only one coming from the East Coast—in no small part due to the inconvenience it caused people, I suppose. In any case, it was good and challenging work, and I enjoyed it; I also loved San Francisco. We'd done more than a few vacations out that way with the kids and had friends that lived there, and I always enjoyed visiting. Not that I was leaving the office much, but it was a great town for restaurants and bars—and even better to be there on an expense account!

I would be remiss if I also didn't mention my team during this "interesting" project we were on. It was during a time that I personally was going through a lot of stuff and I would come to appreciate having the full support of those that were working with me (and let's be honest, supporting me) during that time. It's one thing to be with people all the time at work and after, like Bob and Simon in Chicago, but it's another to be doing that with people when you are traveling 3 timezones away, going through a separation and trying to manage that while also dealing with the client we had at the time, then also being pulled into help sell one of the largest deals that your company was pursuing. At that time I was fortunate enough to have a great team, but also great leaders with me to help manage the chaos and ones that I would work with and bring with me on that "largest deal" I just mentioned once it was done. The cliche'd "who you want in the foxhole with you" comes to mind. Jenn and Jenna were great to have there to help with everything but it was also very rewarding to see how they were growing their careers and "trying" to help them through the challenges, the opportunities, the highs and the lows we all faced.

The Chicago-Based Quick-Serve Restaurant Story: Splitting Time Between San Francisco And Chicago For The "Big Pitch"

My VP at the Bay Area beauty brand was also working on something really big in Chicago around the time we won the beauty brand work. It was quite secretive, but was going to be involving eCommerce and mobile app work, so he wanted me to also help out with the pursuit. It didn't take long until we figured out it was for a pretty important QSR based in the city. And it definitely was a *huge* opportunity: we were looking at a billion-dollar, five-year deal that would have this QSR outsource (essentially rebadge) a huge portion of their digital talent to the French consulting firm. The story of the deal was that one day the CEO and CIO realized that the company's superpowers really were in building restaurants and making burgers: not owning all the tech behind it.

However the thought had occurred to them, they decided to have the French firm and two other huge consulting firms bid on the opportunity to not only help run the technology behind the golden arches, but also take on 800+ new employees from the QSR as part of it. This was a huge tech deal, but it also had huge personnel implications.

Forty People In A Windowless Room For Three Months

This wasn't the most glamorous of pursuits, that's for sure. Our VP, Ted, was quite adamant (and I agreed with him) that he needed to make the possible work we were looking at very secretive, and not operate by the rules. The pursuit was given a codename and was supposed to be all very hush hush. He and one of North American leaders, Tim, would commence flying in over forty of us every week to a windowless room at our office in Chicago right next to O'Hare. This meant that I would start cutting my time in San Francisco shorter and hitting Chicago on my way back to Pittsburgh. It was definitely fast and furious, trying to get as much intel as possible and assess what we would potentially be getting into with this "acquisition." We had little to no access to the client. There was a lot of hypothesis-driven assessment work (even before I found out about hypothesis-driven work at the large MBB firm, which comparatively seemed to be on steroids!) and lots of inter-actions that needed to happen leading up to the final pitch.

Knowing When There Will Be No Value Added And To Walk Away

It was a very interesting dynamic. It felt as if everyone started around the same time every day, gathering in that windowless room to get our marching orders, which were typically translated to us by our "pursuit lead" from our VP. We'd huddle in small groups all day, mainly with some larger groups working in the main room, then everyone would be expected to huddle again in the room at end of day to report on progress then keep working into the night.

This is where I really started to notice that long hours give diminishing returns at some point. You can only keep people there so long, giving them food and making them stay busy, until there are either mistakes or burnout that creeps in. I am sure many people will disagree with me on this, but I was always of the mind to work smarter, not harder. The research out around this as I write in 2025 really backs this up, and even seems to show that we often get more creative ideas while *away* from our desks.

This is where I was thankful I wasn't higher up in the organization: I wasn't the lead, so I didn't have to suffer through everything like my boss did. In the beginning, you would be held waiting for an indeterminate amount of time, never knowing when an update was coming. This was thrilling and all, but I learned to stop giving a shit after a while.

Running Into An Old Friend Or "I Think We Will Be Bringing Jamie To More Meetings...."

While the majority of us peons were being kept back in the windowless room building, as fate would have it, I was invited to a meeting at the Chicago-based QSR's HQ. My group was to include some VPs and one or two other people at my level. As we waited for the QSR's people to join us we took our seats, and they started filing in one-by-one. Shockingly, someone from my time at the Indian firm appeared: my good friend and trench-buddy from the worst project I'd seen there! Now he was one of the leaders of their mobile app platform—small world, indeed.

We couldn't believe it when we saw each other: that after all these years we'd bump into each other on something like this. Technically, he was with the design firm at the time I was at the Indian firm, but we were handling the same client and had to work together a lot through some intense deadlines and insane demands. At this point we had a true bond, and we knew each other "got it." After pleasantries were exchanged, my VP took keen notice of our relationship, and the banter we had, along with our discussion. I noticed I got invited to a lot more meetings after this.

Bringing Humor And Humanity To A Sales Pitch

As we approached the final pitch to the QSR for this big opportunity, the daily sessions in the windowless office increased in time and intensity. I fully wasn't expecting to be in the final pitch. Only several of us could be, and I was there mainly to help prep for the final push.

After they did the dry run through the presentation, I made a bold move and told the VPs and others in the room that I felt that our presentation, though it was good, would be viewed at the same level as other consulting firms with our delivery: why not punch it up with some humor, or differentiate ourselves in some other way? Most of the people in our pitch from the client would be re-badged to our company, or at least work with us and have this huge, literally-billion-dollar decision over their heads. The least we could do would be to make it entertaining! We didn't want to come off as just lecturing the presentation to them with little to no interaction.

I should give credit to our VP in charge, though: he heard me out and told me to get to work with the consultants building the presentation with humor in it. I don't know what had gotten into me and why I was so adamant about it, but apparently the passion had been strong enough to sell our VP on trusting me to do it. Still, there was the problem that I was writing material to make basically fun of ourselves, but I still wouldn't be in the room to deliver it.

Well, that VP decided to include me in the final pitch. It's something I'll never forget. I fully credit this VP with the foresight to see that we did, in fact, need something to differentiate us, and his and the others' openness in allowing jokes to be made ever-so-slightly at their expense. It surely lightened the moment of the presentation. A good friend told me later that I'd basically just been an emcee and comic relief, and I couldn't disagree. We also got a lot of feedback from the client that our presentation was the one that stood out most and had the most character. What can I say? It helped win a billion-dollar deal that's still generating value today.

We Won The Deal

"We Ordered *How Many* Cheeseburgers On The Mobile App?"

Some of my fondest memories were when we would gather at the French firm's office after we won the Chicago-based QSR deal. With the company moving to their new headquarters in downtown Chicago, we'd definitely need to expand our presence there, too, to include all the firm's and the QSR's staff involved in the deal, as well as the newly-formed digital acceleration group that was on the way. We were working on this around the time that Uber Eats, DoorDash, and the other food delivery apps were just getting started, with the dominant force being Uber Eats.

As part of the celebration, and also in some way to test the mobile app, we ordered over a hundred burgers to be delivered. I think we may have separated the order, placing it with different people at different locations of the QSR, so we could go ahead without overwhelming any single one. This was the beginning of a gigantic partnership for us. It would come with its share of ups and downs, but it was exciting, and excitingly challenging, nonetheless. Online delivery was on its way now, and within a few short years it would gain importance in our lives that we could never have imagined.

The Building Of A Team

We signed the deal, and so concluded my first tour of duty helping this QSR with their international digital rollouts to certain markets. After that, I transitioned to a more product-focused role on digital commerce and loyalty. It's also where I and many of my coworkers from the French firm started recruiting talent, both insourced and outsourced, to start coming onto the account.

We were looking for a smart-and-hungry team that just wanted to "get after it." I was very fortunate to recruit and build a team over time that was 1) fantastic to work with, and 2) a group I could also learn from. I was also blessed with some significant relationships and air cover from management that allowed me to be left alone more to explore areas with my own initiative and take opportunities where I found them. Others, and some that I recruited there, weren't so lucky, unfortunately being stuck under some real dictator types. You know the kind: to them, you're never in the office for enough hours—you should always answer the phone when they call—and most of all, you need to give them real information they can share with their superiors to make them look good, smart, and pretty-smelling. It's a hamster wheel with people like that. They're so bloodthirsty to climb the corporate ladder that they'd practically sell their first-born to get there.

It took the recent life experience of divorce to really take stock of what I was trying to do in my life with regard to my career. Why was I continuing to try to live up to someone else's expectations only for their benefit? After really going out on a limb to express myself and get our presentation changed to win the big Chicago QSR deal, I was emboldened to try that more in life and in career. This helped with the overall attitude I shared with my team. Yes, it was serious, and we needed to get stuff done, but I didn't expect people to be there at crazy hours or just "grinding" with me constantly looking over their shoulders. I was changing, and that attitude carried through. Also, I was placing an importance on getting together as a team outside of work, which was highly effective. As a result, we tended to do really good work and enjoy it while doing it—most of us, anyway.

Like the "Bay Area Beauty" project previously mentioned, I had brought Jenn and Jenna along for the ride but would also be paired up with Steve who could help me manage the ever growing team at the time. Steve was older than me, not that it matters, but I really learned a lot from him. He was a good sounding board for me and others, but also came with his own deep experience over time and was good with making sure he could add the more senior gravitas when it came to not only helping out our team but also the client. In consulting you are always appreciative of the individuals you have working with you that don't need a lot of handholding and love to see them grow and flourish on their own. I was lucky to have that mainly on this project with our team.

Discovering The Real Power Of Loyalty And Gamification In A Mobile App

After a while at the Chicago-based QSR, they transitioned me from managing a team of the French firm's international consultants to a more internal role focused on the QSR's Loyalty product. They were going to upgrade the loyalty program and all that came with it— campaigns, offers, incentives, and so on—and this required having a small team to focus on it. It was a great opportunity to learn more about the loyalty ecosystem there, as well as all the players involved, while also being able to to deploy new capabilities in the fast-rising app for the QSR. One of the interesting things people didn't know about the company at the time was that they viewed their competition as *Starbucks* more than the other quick-serve burger chains they seemed most likely to compare themselves to. This makes more sense in light of their getting into the fancy-coffee game later.

The Starbucks angle also meant trying to emulate the loyalty aspects of the Starbucks app, and the gamification that was driving a significant amount of revenue and continued loyalty for the Starbucks app users. Interestingly, though the Chicago-based QSR only launched its app in 2016-2017, the company says it now drives more than 40% of overall revenue. By 2027, the loyalty program alone is expected to contribute over *$45 billion* in annual sales. These are just huge numbers, and it's really cool to think I had a hand in helping that come into being—along with a great team, of course. It's validation that our strategic choices were right.

Conversational Commerce: "Alexa, I Want A Burger And Fries From My Local Burger Spot!"

Another really cool thing that I was able to do while at the Chicago-based QSR was help incubate an idea that was starting to take hold at the time: "conversational commerce." This was the idea of selling goods using the new voice capabilities of products from Amazon and Apple with Alexa and Siri. People weren't engaging then at the level they are now with things like this, but me and a few others were allowed to make the pitch to the QSR's innovation board, along with our great mentor and coach for it, Rick, who would help guide us through the process, to find funding and help us turn this idea into reality.

Years later, this would have broader implications with the rise of large language model (LLM) and AI use-cases that could eventually be incorporated in the drive-through lanes to help with intake and processing of orders. In a recent visit I had to the QSR's Corporate Headquarters I found they now have their own product team for conversational commerce, and they're continuing to use it to explore and test different use cases. Very cool to see!

What we built then with basic algorithms and rules engines looks quaint compared to what's possible now. Modern AI can predict what a customer wants before they know it themselves, altering the offers on display in real-time based on weather, mood, or time of day; probably even their horoscope, if you let it. But the lesson from the Chicago-based QSR is still that the fanciest predictive model in the world means nothing if your operations can't deliver on their promise. Technology velocity, organizational velocity, market velocity—AI just amplifies the gaps between them.

Velocity Vs. Capacity

When we started rolling out new technology features at the QSR, one of the main things that needed constant attention involved what I now call the *Three Velocities Problem.*

We had *Technology Velocity*—how fast our systems could technically handle new features. We could push updates to the app hourly if we wanted. Then we had *Organizational Velocity*—how quickly the huge QSR's thousands of employees could learn, adapt, and support these changes. Spoiler: it wasn't weekly. Finally, there was *Market Velocity*—how fast customers in different regions expected or could handle change. What worked in Chicago might confuse customers in a sleepy rural town.

I figured out after a while that the constant meetings weren't really about capacity; they were more about getting these three different speeds aligned. If you push technology too fast, you break the organization, but if you move too slowly the market could go elsewhere.

This is exactly what companies have to think about with AI today. They can implement ChatGPT tomorrow, but how good will that implementation be—can their people and customers actually use it and get something out of it?

This type of work showed us that what worked in some markets didn't always work in others, and it also gave a really good bird's-eye-view of the political alignments and history of the Chicago-based

QSR—as well as regional leanings or biases when it came to tech. As with any large company, there was a lot of "the way it's always been done" involved when it came to the technology used to transform the company, and this didn't always equate to a speedy process. I was able to go to Canada and London a few times when I was in the international role, but I wish I could have traveled to Asia and Europe more to see how the tech was being used there. Maybe the next go-around, right?

PMO, Boots On The Ground, Real Experience Vs. Fancy Slides

As with a lot of large companies, many consultants worked at the Chicago-based QSR. Starting at the top, you had your management consulting and strategy companies that depended on where the C-suite had the strongest relationships (the MBB companies of McKinsey, BCG, and Bain). Then you had those execution consulting companies (like Capgemini, Deloitte, Accenture); you had the managed service-heavy firms (like Wipro, TCS, and Infosys) then you had digital design-focused agencies. Then there were smaller, more specifically-focused agencies that worked on certain more minor things, or perhaps had a friend at the client company that was trying them out.

Over time at the big QSR, it started becoming more clear that there was a disconnect with the MBB firms trying to dictate how the people in the trenches should work or how the PMO needed to be run versus those of us who were living it every day. We were eventually able to convince management that we needed less and less oversight from those disconnected from the reality of what was really happening in the markets when it came to this digital transformation.

I had been watching different consulting firms clash because they were deployed at the wrong phase. The expensive lesson was: match firm capabilities to project phase, or potentially waste millions on the wrong expertise at the wrong time. I developed a "Consulting Firm Selection Process" on the basis of my experiences:

Strategy Phase

- Best fit: MBB firms (McKinsey, BCG, Bain)
- What they typically do well: Business case development, market analysis, C-suite buy-in
- What they typically don't do: Detailed technical architecture, hands-on implementation
- Potential red flag: They promise to "stay through execution" (they'll staff it with juniors)

Design Phase

- Best fit: Specialized boutiques, niche experts (like the California-based design and consulting firm for UX)
- What they typically do well: Deep user expertise, customer research
- What they typically don't do: Broad strategic vision, large-scale program management
- Red flag: They claim expertise in everything (they don't)

Execution Phase

- Best fit: Big integrators (Accenture, Capgemini, Deloitte)
- What they typically do well: Large teams, program management, vendor coordination
- What they typically don't do: Challenge the strategy enough, value realization
- Red flag: They're still "refining requirements" in month 6

Optimization Phase

- Best fit: Managed services firms (Wipro, TCS, Infosys) or in-house teams
- What they typically do well: Cost efficiency, Business-As-Usual (BAU)-type work, incremental improvements
- What they typically don't do: Transformation, innovation, strategic pivots
- Red flag: They resist any changes to established processes (especially recommendations from outside firms)

The Overlap Strategy: Run Strategy and Design in parallel with different firms. Bring Execution firms in during Design phase for feasibility input. Never let Strategy firms control Execution budgets.

A key question to consider is, are you hiring this firm because they're good at this phase, or because you already have a relationship with them?

Our work with the Chicago-based QSR was one of the few times where both we and the client united in a common goal to just "let us cook," as they say, so we could deliver the best value for the markets and the end user. As I'll describe later, I think there's a balance needed in large organizations when it comes to the type of consultancies that should be engaged, and at what stage. They all promise to do everything, but they rarely do—and if they do try to do everything, you rarely get the best people and effort for your investment.

Chapter Takeaways: Adventures In Different Brands, And Making Huge Deals

1. Bet On The Underdog And Build The Damn Thing
The French consulting firm was falling behind in eCommerce, but the whiteboard challenge from leadership opened a door. I helped build the path through it.

2. Be Useful, Not Important
At the Dallas-based QSR, I ditched ego and jumped into the spreadsheets. This kind of humility forged trust, deep product insight, and early momentum on an account that mattered.

3. Real Leadership Doesn't Flee or Flatter
The hives, the sick pitches, the disappearing "savant"—I endured all of this, and a little more. When actual emotional intelligence and a caring mindset appeared in a mentor like my old boss Pete, it raised my standard for what leadership should feel like.

4. Speak The Truth, Even When It's Unpopular
I warned against a "big bang" launch at the Bay Area beauty brand and they called me a dinosaur. They ignored the warning, burned millions, and had to roll it back. The logic was sound. Experience can help in ways you might never imagine with important decisions.

5. Humor, Humanity, And Winning A Billion-Dollar Deal
I punched up the final pitch to the Chicago-based QSR with humor, and set our presentation apart with it. This kind of differentiation helped win the room and the deal.

6. Build The Team You Wish You'd Had
   When I was given some autonomy, I created a crew driven by energy, trust, and shared purpose. I ditched the "grind" playbook and built a culture that delivered real results, without having to burn people out.

7. Legacy Lives In Loyalty
   From gamified app features to experiments with conversational commerce, I helped plant seeds that now drive literally billions in revenue for the Chicago-based QSR. I helped launch these features and shift customer behavior.

CHAPTER 8

The Hidden Cost of Prestige: When a Dream Job Becomes a Slow Burnout

It was around the two- or two-and-a-half-year mark that I was rolled off the Chicago-based QSR as they were starting to work out the economics and either bring in cheaper talent or offshore more and more of the onshore delivery team. I was fine with it—I was ready to move on to new challenges and new experiences. I didn't realize at the time that this would inadvertently set up my next career stop at an MBB firm.

While having dinner with a longtime friend from Wharton in Palo Alto, the discussion came around to what I was doing at the French consulting firm. After I finished telling him about it, he asked me if I'd be interested in talking with his employer, one of the MBB firms, since they had acquired a company in Pittsburgh and were establishing a beachhead there for the design- and tech-leaning practice they were building. I was flattered he thought I could even *work* for this company, but I politely declined, as I was happy at the French firm and managing changes in life at the time that needed my attention: namely, divorce, and how best to manage that, while still managing my career. After a few more discussions with him and others, I did realize two things: A) The brand on my resume would be a game-changer when it came to those brands people looked to for help with career trajectory and growth, and B) It would mean less time on the road, as they had an office near where I lived, and were looking to establish a culture for this fast-growing group of around 100 to 150 people that would be looked at as the tech professionals.

The MBB firm had acquired a technology consulting company to accomplish this. It was sort of like a startup with a very rich uncle (there is that phrase again) that was looking to shake things up, but also a group the firm could turn to as the experts when it came to the technology "cases" (projects) they were pitching to companies. After going through a very lengthy and dragged-out recruiting process—the original "handler" quit, and I was left in limbo for quite some time—I finally received an offer to join. Wharton had taught me in Executive Education negotiation classes to never leave money on the table, as the worst they might say is no, so I negotiated with them on salary and soon landed a role as a Principal in the company, which was growing quickly. It was an exciting time, and the next step in growing my career, but the most important thing was that I was going to be able to continue learning—and now in a *very* accelerated, new way.

I Have To Go Into An Office In Pittsburgh For The First Time In Ten Years And Not An Airport?

One of the bigger adjustments I had to make was getting back to commuting by car into an office downtown for the first time in ten years. I had been just on autopilot to and from the airport, week after week, to jet off to a city to do my consulting work, but now I would be fighting traffic every day and managing the stress of the commute—parking and dodging weather as I would get to the office, only to then make sure I was at my desk for a certain amount of hours. Looking back now, it feels crazy to me how arbitrary and soul-sucking that practice is. To be fair, it was a great office with great people; it just wasn't very busy at the time, as we were in growth mode (this meant lots of travel for everyone), and we definitely were a small office for this large MBB firm compared to the others. As I would find out after six months of doing this, it wasn't going to last *too* long, as the onset of Covid would force us all into the new way of working that seems so common now.

What Is Our eCommerce Strategy?

Once I landed at the MBB firm in their tech consultancy, I was eager to discover what this very prestigious company had in place when it came to eCommerce strategy.

Not much, it turned out.

What I quickly saw was that firm was great at convincing companies through the numbers and business cases that investing in eCommerce was well worth it, like they did for the large MRO company I worked with, but then when it came to the strategy and execution of how best to roll out eCommerce at these companies, it made more sense and was more cost-effective to have the mid-to-low-tier consulting firms do it. This led to constant internal questioning: how far down did we want to go when it came to implementing these types of things? And not just in eCommerce, but also in implementing other technologies?

I was able to network in with a small group of "experts" at the company over time, and this would become our eventual eCommerce group that would help define the firm's eCommerce strategy, vision, materials, and positioning. My main responsibility was delivering value no matter what the case was or the tech was, but I was very passionate about the eCommerce area given my background. In the beginning, it was rough: I was something new for this MBB company as an organization, and they didn't have a huge amount of experience with people like me—which unfortunately meant I was less marketable internally for being staffed on projects. The ones I *was* staffed on were usually well outside of my realm of expertise, but that just meant I got to learn a lot more about other tech areas, which I enjoyed, even though at times it was pretty stressful.

Of course, unbeknownst to me, the Covid pandemic was going to be declared after I'd worked here for only half a year, and my world—along with everyone else's—was about to become bonkers, leading to me working on multiple cases for over two years straight with little to no breaks as the world shifted very rapidly to ordering daily things online. eCommerce was on a rocket ship to the center of our universe, as we were all about to find out.

Covid And New Ways Of Working

Covid forced our office to evacuate just after I'd begun to get to know people there. Lockdown also happened to start the week my fiancée Catherine moved in with me in Pittsburgh! We survived and thrived, I'm happy to say, and ended up getting married. We both figured if you could make it through lockdown, you could make it through anything.

The saving grace for me was that we had a house where we could easily have two offices, and the kids were with us every other week. The other saving grace was that, after 15 years of consulting on the road, I was well equipped technically and mentally to work from anywhere. All those years had prepared me well—including the fact that I had a home office already set up for the weeks or days when I didn't travel. So the transition was easy for me, but I came to realize this was not the case for others I worked with. They had big families, or no home offices, or houses ripped up from renovation, or shared apartments with roommates—lots of different scenarios were playing out that wouldn't enable good work environments. I considered myself very lucky. It's funny to think how that professor I had back at

Dayton, with his offline and asynchronous working style and homework assignments enabled by the early internet had accidentally prepared me for remote work.

I would be remiss if I didn't mention the outstanding leadership at the MBB firm during this time. Especially at the top with our chairman Joe. The empathy and compassion from him during this crazy time in history was a masterclass in how real leaders approach really hard times. It was my first time in a business setting where a leader showed real tears to his employees about everything our company and people were going through. I don't know if it was planned, but I remember him making sure there were frequent all company zooms to communicate to us all the things that were happening across our company, and I remember specifically one zoom call happening from his daughters room (was pink and he pointed that out) and he would tell us about all the struggles even his own family was going through. It was heartfelt and sincere and in those times I know our whole company was rallied around him because he was being vulnerable and sincere. He and the leadership did what was right for our company for sure. Between things like ordering monitors and keyboards to giving a stipend to everyone to equip their home gyms if they chose. Along with all the gift cards for uber eats, etc. it was definitely a defining moment at the company and one that was met head on by leadership and not just ignored.

"You Want Me To Just Make Slides?" Did I Make The Right Choice?

I had been at the major MBB firm a while; I was working with some great people, and was able to work on some really cool, groundbreaking cases. It's not too often you get to help on a case where you assess companies to be bought or sold for billions of dollars based on the work you're doing. That said, I noticed a few things.

The first was that it was all about slide making. Slides were the currency at this company. The most frustrating part of this was that their quality was completely subjective. I would have Partners or Principals rip my slides for things like "too many words," but then they would turn around and create slides with *double* my word count.

In fairness, there was an art and a science to it, and I did learn a lot about slide-making. I didn't realize how much I had learned on this subject, as well as storytelling in a minimalist but still impactful way, until I was out of the organization.

The second, and bigger issue, was that there were not a lot of client interactions and chances to sell. Sure, we had the occasional times when the Partners would be on the brink of selling a project, but when pressed and asked who at the firm had done this before, they would typically turn to people like me and my peers to help them sell the project and convince the client we knew what we were doing.

Hands down, my story of the large MRO company is the one I repeat the most, and when I look back through all these years it definitely was one of the most transformative. (This is closely-followed by the Chicago-based QSR.) So the client-facing aspect of the job and the selling part, these being two of my big strengths, really weren't opportunities for me at the MBB firm. Hence, by review time, it came down to critiquing people on consulting skills and slide making. Something I would also learn later after leaving was that all the "extra credit" projects I had done, thinking it would help my career, did nothing for me in that aspect. You know the ones: thought leadership, panel here, panel there, mentoring, extra business development support. Hell, I was even the office lead for my technical group at the firm when I was canned, so that shows how much that "extra credit" stuff is really valued.

Strategy Vs. Execution

While I was getting a masterclass on the strategy side of things, and learning a huge amount, I definitely was missing the execution and sales side of things. Typically after our assessment we would be handing off to another group, the client company, or in some rare cases finding ourselves embedded with another consulting firm that was executing—which was always awkward. But I wasn't getting to do some of the things I had done before: not only regarding the strategy, but also the design and definition phases that would then set up the teams for the implementation and the thrill of the hunt with sales. The positive was that I would be exposed to a lot of scenarios. The negative was that after several weeks you would move on to the next thing. Lots of starts and stops.

The strategy-versus-execution divide at the MBB firm feels especially relevant now that everyone wants an "AI strategy." I see similar disconnects: beautiful slides about transformative AI use cases, followed by nothing. No implementation plan or change management, or no consideration of whether their data is even clean enough to feed to an AI model. It's like planning a Mars mission when you haven't figured out how to fuel the rocket. The consultants selling AI transformation today are making the same mistake we made with digital transformation—forgetting that strategy without proper execution, or not including people with the scars who have implemented it before, is just expensive hallucination.

Learning Your Strengths: What You're Good At. Marcus Buckingham: Double Down On Strengths

One of the big things I noticed at the large MBB firm was that reviews/feedback often came up, and they typically revolved more around your Areas For Development, or "AFDs," rather than your strengths (at least that was the perception by me and others). I never could understand why the culture was like this; too many A-type personalities, I guess. I often thought back to a very transformative talk and speaker I had seen live at Wharton named Marcus Buckingham. The gist of his talk had been around believing in yourself and your strengths, and how you should double down on your strengths.

Of course there would be times you would need to improve in certain areas and develop new skill sets, but he emphasized that we should stay focused on the strengths we knew we had. After years of being told the areas I was deficient in at this company, I was starting to wake up to the fact that these people telling me where I needed to improve probably had their own insecurities they were dealing with—and were also being constantly told where they were deficient themselves. I was also realizing that I wasn't in an environment or situation where I could double down on my strengths.

It was a vicious cycle. I would typically take the feedback but often ignore the AFD part, and as the years went on, I became more and more jaded against this practice. There was also a big shift in the MBB firm. The company had new leadership, and they were chopping up our now 300-person-strong tech consultancy group and putting some people with a newly-minted digital group under a new name while us others would stay with an older group. This effectively killed our culture, and a lot of people weren't happy about it.

And not only that—it ratcheted up the microscope on people,

AFDs, and billability, all in a move to start cutting people. It was a course-correct from the massive hiring that had led up to and gone on during Covid, and the means to justify letting people go was originally the AFD area. I could see the writing was on the wall: eCommerce projects weren't popping up like they used to, I wasn't getting staffed, our review roundtables were turning toxic where people were fighting to keep their mentees employed—it wasn't looking good. I fought the good fight as long as I could, and was actually billable on a case when my advisor informed me I was on a performance action plan and would be receiving remedial coaching.

I look back on that now and I'm thankful for it happening: it was like a huge weight off my chest. However, unknown to my advisor and others, someone from my past at the MBB firm had luckily reached out months before with a revolutionary offer: why not invest in yourself and use your time at the company as a runway to build something where you won't have to rely on a corporation to define who you are and what success looks like?

The Hatchet Falls

And so I was eventually "transitioned" out of the firm: that infamous word the top consulting firms use to make sure they don't pop up in the press with that even nastier word, "layoffs."

I thought it was quite apparent that I had needed to fit into a certain bucket for things to work out for me there, but in actuality it came down to numbers: they just needed a way to go about making the cuts. That, coupled with the goal posts constantly being moved on me and my remedial assigned coach, led me to plainly see things were heading a certain way. Then, of course, at my next check-in with my advisor, the HR rep happened to be there, too. It was time to go up to non-MBB-Firm Heaven, apparently. I was informed of my performance on my most recent review: it wasn't up to the standard that the company wanted. The interesting thing was that the review was never shared with me, and I had to work through HR to officially get it released to me. I think I read it only once. Whether it's me just blocking it out now, or me thinking at the time this was the narrative they needed to spin to make a reduction, I didn't care. I was billable, and I had testimonials from some pretty high up political Partners to help my case. In fact, some were pretty surprised when I told them I was being transitioned. Maybe they were bullshitting me, but I still appreciated it.

In the end it didn't matter. I was an easy target—someone niche in a place that wanted more generalism, someone who questioned authority and wasn't as tied in to the political heavy hitters as they should have been—but ultimately, too, someone who was unwilling to change or ignore those strengths I knew I had and wanted to double down on.

Looking back now, I'm very glad I was one of the early ones. It started me down a path that really helped me love myself more, and it's also been a path that helped me create the space I needed to help me to help others. Since that time, I've had countless people from the firm and elsewhere reach out to me to ask me about my journey. They ask how I got over it, how I gained clarity about what to do, and how it led me to the situation I am in today. For this, I am thankful. As you'll also see later, I'm a proud alumni of this company, with them as my client—again, even after all these years, after having first started with them as a client at Wharton! I really value the time, the learning, and the relationships I built there.

Investing In Myself With Coaching And Getting LLC-Approved

One of the biggest and best decisions I made when I knew where things were about to go at the firm was taking a call with an old colleague from it, Matt, who had started in the same class I did. Matt was only at the MBB firm for two years before leaving. I even worked a case with him as a co-lead. I had never experienced this before, but while all of us were chained to our laptops, in constant meetings, grinding on slides, this man Matt was hardly online. I would reach out for some things, either on slack or by email, and it would often be at least a day until I heard back from him.

What the hell was he doing?

But I'll tell you what he was doing, which he told me about later: Matt had secretly been building his coaching business and was living by the principles he espoused. One of the biggest and best was taking a radical approach to "creating space." Looking back on it now, we were all the proverbial frog in the pot, not noticing as the water got ever-closer to boiling. Matt was lucky enough to discover at the firm that he needed to just not enter the pot. He said it came at great cost to finally get to this realization; he'd been part of this race for a long time, but he woke up to realize he was meant to serve others. What better way to do this than by investing in himself with coaching and mentoring, but also then putting what he was learning into real action?

One of the first steps was creating space for himself. It was nothing crazy: just things like not logging into email or messaging first thing when you woke up, and not looking at work or digital "things" in the evening, maybe say after dinner. It was also things like aggressively blocking your calendar—which, by the way, I learned after a few years at the MBB firm was actually a practice taught to the Partners there in their executive training.

Again, this was nothing Earth-shattering, but even on my own journey, it was hard to put into practice. We were taught to believe for so long that if you weren't online and able to respond to messages immediately, you were of little to no value to your employer. How wrong that is! Even if it has, yes, taken me over twenty five years to get to that realization. I learned more about Matt's journey and how he employed his practices in his own life later once I started coaching with him, but it still fascinates (and saddens) me that even as I write this, we both know former colleagues silently suffering, lacking a clear idea about their goals and direction, and in some extreme cases even having burnout so severe that hospital or doctors' visits were required.

It's You, Not Us

I was unsure if I even wanted to tackle this part of my journey when I wrote this book. They do say, after all, that it's not good to dwell on the past. Going into the past might only result in resentments: I'm sure you've heard some of the mantras.

But after more reflection, sharing my thoughts at a recent coaching retreat and getting encouragement from others who had gone to the extreme in terms of working, burnout and now starting recovery, I would be remiss not to visit what had happened leading up to me being let go from this large company in hopes it can help others get the clarity they need.

As mentioned previously, the big firms tend to really want to try to keep their names out of the press with the word "layoffs," so leading up to the day I was let go, it just felt more and more like the deck was stacked against me. You would be told about multiple areas for development, and to address them—then you'd start addressing them, get feedback on addressing them from peers and Partners, and then once you thought you were ticking those boxes and moving on, the goal posts would move and there would be a whole *new* set of areas for development to address. No matter how much feedback you gathered in support of addressing those, it would just be deemed "not good enough."

This is an ego blow: you spend your entire career trying to please your employer, usually getting good feedback from people you report to and work with, and suddenly you're being told you're not good enough. It's hard. I used to view it as the "it's not us, it's you" inversion, and I'd really end up beating myself up over it.

The actual damage done when you internalize like this is huge. It ends up in causing you a lot of stress, and often we don't realize that by a certain point, the damage is done, the narrative is set, and the die is cast. There are diminishing returns, and it's best to recognize it's a business decision that ended it for you: nothing you did or didn't do was a factor (unless it's an extreme factor). Money was tight, they needed to make cuts, and you happened to be one of them.

I will forever be grateful to the Partner who did finally reach out to me to share the real hard news like this, rather than the tale that was being spun by others on why I was being let go. I am also grateful for the countless hours of listening by my peers and others as they tried to be helpful to me in the downward spiral that was being laid off. Some were very shocked, or at least feigned to be, that I was being let go—others could only listen and, I imagine, think *better him than me*, and others viewed me talking about what was happening as just a case of being bitter. Funnily enough, many of those people were then let go a year or two later or decided to take early retirement because things had gotten so crazy.

I realize now that the large MBB firm was in fact right. It *was* me and not them. I wasn't being the person, partner, Dad, friend, and colleague I really wanted to be because my perceived value, by me and what I perceived was by others, was tied up in this company and what I thought its brand meant, and it took this painful journey and reflection to realize I wasn't their material, but more importantly I wasn't being myself by following that playbook. But the biggest "unlock"—where I might give a small wink at all those consulting people—was that the company wasn't fitting me, either, and where I wanted my life to go, as well as who I was becoming while there. It was a crescendo of time, work, stress, and so on taking its toll, where I was all about the employer and pleasing them, and a lot less about me and others in my life. I wasn't present, and was doing all those bad habits outlined above, all in the pursuit of what an employer thought success was—not what I thought it was. I realize now I was lucky as an early one to be transitioned out.

One of the people in the Pittsburgh office said it best: "I don't value-map to this company anymore." Over time it would just get worse: not only here at the firm, but at a lot of other firms. As more and more people learned my story, they have reached out over time for advice on how I approached things and got clarity in what I wanted to do afterward, and how they should approach what they see as their crisis point driving them to either look elsewhere or take a radically different approach to work. It amazes me, how many of these people think that just keeping their head down and producing for their corporate overlord is going to work out fine in the end, without realizing they need to create space themselves to do their own self-work and self-investment if they want to really get the clarity they seek in their lives.

Micromanagement

We've all been there; we've all had those bosses, peers and others in our work lives (and sometimes personal lives) that seem to need to look over your shoulder, have multiple check-ins a day, make sure their feedback is incorporated, and so on.

This is toxicity in its purest form. Those people are typically inse-cure and unsure of their work and how much the company values them, so they do everything in their power to project their insecuri-ties onto you. This also typically rears its head when you're dealing with those people who aren't open-minded, and think they either know best or are always the smartest ones in the room.

It's best to identify these people early on and try to create space between you and them—so take the time to establish that contract with yourself. For example, things like: family and friends come first; I will only be logging in and out at these times; if it's an emergency you have permission to call or text me. Nothing Earth-shattering, but simple decisions or barriers that protect the things you value. At some point you can even discuss it with your boss or plant those seeds yourself. This establishes that you do in fact value yourself, your health and well-being, and when that happens you are present and bringing the best version of yourself to your employer. And how could they not want that?

I once had a boss who was miffed that I couldn't stay late for something, or had to leave early for something, as a result of a situ-ation arising with my kids. It wore on me, creating undue stress and other bad feelings, and I stewed on this for days until finally I had to talk to him about it. In my next scheduled one-on-one I told him my family was my first priority, and that if things like leaving early for a doctor's appointment for a kid were going to be an issue, then basically he was going to have to deal with it. It took a lot of courage to say that, but I couldn't keep it inside anymore—and no, I really hadn't thought through the consequences too much.

It's hard sometimes, isn't it? Especially when your kids are involved. But I realize now that he respected me for that, and our relationship was different from that day forward. I even ended up working with this person again later.

🔑 Chapter Takeaways: When Prestige Isn't Peace

1. Big Names Don't Guarantee Big Alignment
   The large MBB firm had the brand, the cachet, and the clout, but inside, it ran on a playbook that fit neither my strengths nor my soul. I was hired to build value: not make perfect slides to no real benefit of anyone.

2. Covid Changed Everything, Including Me
   The pandemic forced a new mode of working that was bad for a huge amount of people, but not for me. It gave me useful new perspective: "being here now" is more important than being productive, and it feels really meaningful to design my life on my own terms.

3. A Culture Obsessed With Deficiency Will Drain You
   At the MBB firm, every review zeroed in on AFDs, or Areas for Development, but "coaching" like this really grinds you down and, at least sometimes, can pull you away from your awareness of your own strengths. I didn't want to forget them: I wanted to double down on them.

4. Letting Me Go Set Me Free
   The MBB firm layoff came cloaked in polite language and HR process, but it was an unexpected gift: I didn't have to keep trying to contort myself into a mold that was never made for me.

5. Investing In Yourself Is Non-Negotiable
   Reconnecting with Matt and stepping into coaching was about reclaiming space, vision, and the agency to choose my path going forward.

6. Micromanagement Is Fear Disguised As Leadership
   I saw firsthand how control is often a mask for insecurity. I stopped apologizing for boundaries—and started writing contracts for myself that honored what mattered most, even if I didn't always explicitly state this to my employer.

7. It Was Me, And That Was the Win.
   I didn't fit the MBB firm because I was evolving, and the old definition of success no longer applied. Leaving was the start of finally living in alignment with my own values.

CHAPTER 9

From Layoff to LLC: The Unconventional Path to Building Something Actually Yours

Starting An LLC

As mentioned earlier, one of the best investments I've made was coaching with Matt. It was investing in myself and partnering with someone to hold me accountable. If I hadn't have done this, I wouldn't be where I am now, with an LLC, writing this book and reflecting back on the journey that got me here. You really don't realize it when you're in it. I remember being out of the MBB company about seven or eight months and catching up with a Partner still at it who I had done some great work with, and after giving him the update on me, he stopped and said, "Wow, you really *have* done a lot! It's amazing to hear your journey and all that you've got going on!" I was dumbfounded: here I was thinking I was a failure, being unsure of myself and feeling like I had no semblance of a plan.

But I just didn't have the right perspective. I was living the entrepreneurial dream (and sometime-hell) every day, not knowing what was coming next, but really hadn't stepped back to realize that I had come a long way on a pretty unique journey. Here was a very successful Partner of this major company, listening to me commenting on how far along and diversified I seemed to be since leaving the "corporate shackles" behind. Something I would find as I spoke to more people from the MBB firm was that they envied where I was at. They envied my situation, and that felt very confirming! Here I had the freedom to do what I wanted, and *when* I wanted, and they realized their lives were reduced to things like making sets of slides and constantly being judged on them.

On the flip side, I was a little jealous of their paychecks and health benefits—but after listening to how these employees pined to be gone some day from their current situation, I realized I was better off. I would figure this out.

The Power Of Being In A Group In The Same Situation (Other Entrepreneurs)

I didn't realize it at the time, but when I signed up for the coaching, it not only was with Matt as my coach, but also a group of people in somewhat similar situations. We had some dealing with corporate burnout, others with ageism, and others with trying to balance being a Mom or Dad and being present for your family with a high-intensity work environment. It was a group of people that were all going through transformative times in their lives. It didn't matter what they were thinking of doing next—though this coaching and group sessions did help focus that—but looking back on it now, and still doing the program currently, the biggest benefit was listening to and sharing with other people in similar (and sometimes worse) situations. It was group therapy at its best, and also did great at keeping everyone accountable to help you keep progressing and "stacking those wins," as Matt likes to say.

Self Exploration And Self Discovery

This can be hard for a lot of people, and absolutely was for me. The beauty of seeking out coaching and accountability in the beginning is to help you create the space you need to get clarity on where you are—and, most importantly, to recognize what you've come from and what you never want to go through again. This is often overlooked. Everyone is so focused on the next big thing, be it entrepreneurial, corporate, or something totally different, that they don't really take the time to focus on what they want and will make them happy. So often, you get people that just go right back into the fire and grind of soul-sucking work or other activities, and they accidentally end up in a similar bad situation that they had wanted to escape.

Even when we think we know, or have discovered, our true path, it can still change. And being open to that change can mean a lot. Two and a half years after I started a coaching program, I think I'm now on my third or fourth path—but at least when I look back on it, I was moving forward, not looking back, and also not settling for something that I know wouldn't bring me happiness.

The First Pitches

From an LLC perspective, you finally get to a point where you need to start working the network and making pitches. You refine multiple times and shape it the more you go. Given my sales and business development background, I treated it as "all systems go" from the start, and just tried to land freelance consulting where I could. I started with what we call in coaching "messy offers"—this means, in essence, that you shouldn't wait until your offer is perfect. There's an old saying: " 'perfect' is the enemy of 'good enough'."

Lots of people just wait too long to get their offer perfect, and accidentally kill their momentum in the process. I wasn't going to let that happen for myself. I was hitting the emails, phones, LinkedIn messages, and everything else I could think of on a daily basis; I was managing my own Google Sheets spreadsheet (sometimes I can be a bit old school) of more than 250 active conversations and was hopeful that at least one would land. And finally, only a few months after being officially "transitioned" out of the MBB firm, I got a positive response.

The First Client!

Yes!! Wait, What!? NO! Or, Better Said: The Ups And Downs Of Entrepreneurship

After a long slog of "warm calling" for a few months, I was able to secure an engagement. The work made sense: help a small-to-mid-size firm get more intelligent about the space they wanted to be in by interviewing some folks from my old MBB firm in that area, and more importantly, see if there was a way to get a partnership with that firm or other members of the MBB group, and even maybe go beyond them.

I got to use my consulting skills to quickly get the client what they needed, and was told I'd be paid a very good rate to do it. Things were going so well after the final readout that the client was interested in bringing me on full-time for the remainder of the year and keeping me even longer than that! This was amazing: I wouldn't have to worry as much, and could secure a steady income stream. Life at this point had taught me to not be too excited until I saw the signature on the contract, but I was very confident this was going to happen.

Well, it didn't. I talked with the client over the weekend to get the deal secured on a Monday, but then got a call from my main client contact. They told me she and her colleague who had been helping get the deal done were terminated, and our deal was dead.

This was a kick to the gut. What's more, the President of the company had no idea that these two had had an agreement with me, and I had to negotiate to get even *half* of what I was promised, with the back half being predicated on me getting a partnership signed for them. This was a really good lesson on not putting all your eggs in one basket.

Of course, I hadn't stopped talking with other prospects about potential opportunities, but I had definitely been led to believe for a short while that this one major anchor client was going to solve a lot of problems for me: and that's just not what happened.

The Proliferation Of Referral Agreements

During my short time being independent, the one thing I noticed—and had to learn the hard way—was that a lot of the small-to-midsize companies I worked with could only offer referral agreements in a gesture of good faith. It was harder to sell them on the value being delivered for my time, which makes sense. Particularly in the case of startups just worried about making payroll, companies like these don't often think they have time or money to pay independent consultants. But this often seemed very short-sighted to me—these companies can really benefit from people coming in from larger organizations, ones they typically emulate and want to be like, to give that diversity of perspective and show where value can be added.

These companies are still struggling even now, when, in my mind, it's easy to assess some very big costs: costs of inertia, as well as not acting quicker to get outside help, perspective, and some kind of external force to drive them in a direction or complete a vision they had. There are lots of opportunity costs they either don't see or, at worst, completely ignore.

Leveraging The MBB's Brand, As Well As The French Firm's

To the preceding point, the best part of working at companies like the MBB and the French firm is the vast array of opportunities and situations you get to experience. You are always learning, and always changing your approaches and solutions to problems.

At the French firm, in my experience, it tended to be medium-to-long-term for consulting engagements, which meant more time to learn and get familiar with a single company or two over the course of a year. At the MBB firm it was much faster—you were typically on several different clients through the year or paid for internal work, so there was a lot of exposure, as well as constantly changing direction and learning. Clients couldn't typically afford to pay for the consultants at those rates to endure long cases, but there are exceptions; I have one former colleague from the firm who's been on the same client for about three and a half years.

With my consulting experience, I started in eCommerce-focused consulting, but over time that has evolved to digital supply chain, order management, loyalty management, digital marketing, data governance, data architecture, and so on—so not only was I learning new client situations and problems, but I was also being introduced to new technology challenges and helping to solve them.

Justifying The Cost/Investment/ROI

I remember Matt "selling" me on the coaching program. It was a huge mindshift for me, and even more so when I consider my path from Wharton executive education, where they paid *me* to take executive-education courses. Now I was going to pay someone else out of my own pocket to help coach me and get me through these rough waters?

It took a little convincing by Matt, then me convincing my wife, but I will be forever grateful for the chance I took on it, and the support from my wife to do it. For one, I don't think this book would be anywhere near close to being completed in my lifetime if I had not done that. It's hard to put into words all the benefits that came from Matt's "Corporate Graduation" program, but hands down the one thing I gained from putting "skin in the game" was the motivation to keep pushing myself forward. I recommend some type of coaching or mentorship for everyone, even if you have regular helpful conversations with peers and others you know. It'll be even better if it can be in a group setting—just sharing those stories and hearing what other people go through is immensely helpful. Also, that you're sometimes able to *give* when it comes to advice or coaching on your own in those group settings is what really feels good.

Partnering With People: Stronger Together

Apart from coaching, one of the *other* best things I did to help move me forward was partner with people with experience deeper than my own. These were people all looking to either progress their LLC journey, get a W2 job, or just find a way out of their already-existing nightmare of a W2 job. I was fortunate enough to have a great network, as well as to come upon some individuals also struggling to get clarity on their next steps. It helped advance my thinking, positioning, and offerings a lot more, as well as helped me to get a clear idea of what "next" looked like for myself.

I'm grateful to all those individuals who helped me during my LLC journey to get that clarity. My success also came from getting plugged in with some great startup companies, where there was mutual benefit to having thought-partners and helping them out where I could. When I eventually landed a W2 job I found myself drawing on a lot of the experience I gained in the LLC, more so than my consulting experience. Having those battle scars and experience was invaluable.

Moving To A W2, But On My Terms To Help My New Self

While my LLC experience was invaluable, eventually that runway and the economy dictated the need to get a W2 position for the stability. Funds weren't endless, and I was staring at two kids going to college: I needed to swallow pride and get a steady paycheck. I was going to take a W2, but it was going to be on *my* terms. I wanted to do good work with good people I knew, trusted, and who had seen me at my best. I also realized the value I brought and wanted to make sure that wasn't discounted.

Weighing The Options: Big Company Vs. Small Startup

After constant interviewing and networking on this front for months, and what seemed like an eternity, I ended up with two offers. One was for a very small consulting firm, and one was with a large IT organization. It wasn't an easy decision, but through the help of having Matt there to coach me and work through weighing the options, along with talking it through with my wife and friends, I came to the best decision I could.

The good news was that they were both sales roles: through coaching and self reflection, I realized this was a skill being wasted by the MBB I was at, and something I was good at and wanted to get back into. (Thank you also to Marcus Buckingham!) On one hand, the startup had the upside of being smaller and more nimble, and I would be able to make an impact with decisions that could and would be fast. It also helped that I really liked its President, and had really good conversations with him.

However, it was a lot smaller than firms I had been at in the past, and would be leveraging my network and book of business to open up new doors. One thing I couldn't shake was that if they were relying on *my* network, the salary and options they were willing to give me made me feel it was being highly undervalued. Along with the idea that, really, who knew how long this company would be around given its size?

This, along with what I will explain here, helped me to make the ultimate decision to go to the bigger IT company. It was with people I had worked with previously and had past success with; they were bigger, had more support systems, and had already been established at a lot of the companies where I already had network myself—hence, it made it an easier ask or sale than if I was with some small startup just trying to break in. Add to that I had actually had this company as a client when I was at the MBB firm so was familiar with them and got a lot of good feedback and encouragement to join them from the MBB firm Partners who worked with them.

In the end, it's anyone's guess which would have been better. But I feel that at that stage in my life, I made the right choice.

Taking that W2 position in the age of AI felt different. This time, I went in knowing that half of what we'd build would probably be automated within five years. But that's exactly why they needed someone like me—someone who'd seen entire business models evaporate and rebuild, who knew the difference between fundamental change and temporary disruption. My value was in helping navigate the transition from "the old ways" without losing what actually mattered: the human connections, the institutional knowledge, and the culture that no algorithm could replicate.

Walk And Talk: Increasing The Steps And Conversations (Along With Podcasts)

One of the key things I started to institute was getting out from behind the desk a bit more, whether that be here locally or traveling to see the client. At the MBB, we were all chained to our desks fearing we would miss a message, or people would think we weren't working—it didn't help that the majority of time there was during Covid.

Remember that story about Matt at the MBB? In my new position, I was going to create the space I needed to think strategically, have dedicated focus time, not be distracted by messaging, and so on. And the big thing was that I was going to increase my step count. I noticed when working in Chicago (or any big city) my step counts were way higher than when sedentary at home. With how tethered in we have become with our phones now it made it a bit easier. It was like taking the office with me. I would be able to monitor email, messages etc. while walking and not feel the guilt of not being behind a desk. I would have a lot of work calls while doing this, and the biggest thing I came away with was the feeling of being much more creative and spontaneous while moving.

It didn't have to necessarily be on a call with someone: I would be out there, walking, or better yet "rucking," with a heavy backpack. I'm a big believer in this, and highly recommend the related book *The Comfort Crisis*, by Michael Easter (credit to my Brother-in-law Nick for turning me onto it). At least for myself, I'm able to strategically and creatively solve some problems while being out of the office like that—I'm able to think well on my own. I would use tools like Notion and ChatGPT to process ideas and projects, then when back in the physical office I'd create materials or presentations using that output to help refine them.

There is the concept of "double-counting": in Dan Sullivan's book *Who Not How*, it's said that only around 20% of your creative ideas come from the office. I'll avoid pouring too much detail in here about the double-count system, but it started with the Industrial Revolution and the mindset that we needed to be "clocking in" and "clocking out" every day, working eight-hour shifts for forty hours per week.

The trouble is that some people think that unless you're "working" by physically being somewhere for 40-70 hours a week, then you aren't really working. And it's gotten worse with the more digital devices have taken hold in our lives. You're in the "always on" mindset more than you think. Covid and working from home contributed to this, too. If you didn't have the space or physical and mental boundaries, work might have really eaten you alive at that point.

But being at your desk doesn't always equal work, and being away from your desk doesn't always mean *not* working. And that is a hard mental switch to flip in certain minds. Given my travel and consulting work over the years, I felt like this was a bit easier for me than others to grasp—except during Covid, when circumstances had everyone "always on" for so long that how unhealthy (or simply unnecessary) it was became more obvious on a wider scale.

Double-counting when it comes to working can equate to working out, taking long walks or bike rides, journaling, reading, meditating, building a report at work, or leading a meeting, all while mentally processing a different work-related task. You might spend time away from your desk at work while trying to work out problems, or while still doing *other* necessary things at work. Sometimes you might have ideas for work solutions while doing another work-related task, but they often also come to you in a completely different environment.

When you change your mindset to this and accept it, it's very freeing, and helps you realize you're putting more time into work than you may have thought. It helped me get the clarity I needed to really process what my journey has been, and what I've been through over the years to get me where I am today.

🗝 Chapter Takeaways: The Rebuild Starts With You

1. Perspective Means a Lot
   At first, I felt lost, uncertain, and behind. But when I stepped back from myself, and heard it reflected by others, I saw the truth: I was living something that a lot of people envied. I had (and have) freedom, ownership, and the ability to move. The corporate exit was a fork in the road, but definitely not a failure.

2. Group Reflection Can Accelerate Healing
   Coaching with Matt was a mirror held up by others on similar paths. It was shared pain, yes, and also shared progress. The group became part-therapy, part-momentum engine, and it was all fuel for my next chapter.

3. The First Offer Won't Be the Final One
   My early LLC wins were messy, and that was the point. I didn't wait for perfection, because that takes too long: I shipped, pitched, and learned hard lessons—like dead deals and broken promises. And I just kept moving.

4. Scar Tissue Builds Strategy
   Referral deals, unpaid calls, feeling like the value I brought wasn't being properly priced—this all sharpened my sense

of what works and what's worth it. I drew on my experience with the French firm and the MBB firm to shape something smarter, leaner, and most importantly, mine.

5. Coaching Isn't An Expense—It's Leverage
   The investment felt risky, but it gave me structure, clarity, and a container to build something real. Without the skin in the game, this book, and the life it reflects, might still be stuck in my head.

6. W2 Doesn't Mean Succumbing To The Corporate Shackles
   I returned to corporate without desperation; I knew what I wanted. I knew the deal. This time, I chose my W2 work on my own terms—aligned with my strengths, strategic, and leveraged to help me deliver the best value to them.

7. Movement Makes Meaning
   Walking calls, podcasts, weighted-backpack ruck walks—most of my best thinking was away from a desk, and came with movement. I stopped confusing "being at my desk" with productivity, and started designing a life that served both my work *and* my well-being.

CHAPTER 10

How Your Past Experience Becomes Your Secret Weapon in the AI Revolution

Is ChatGPT And AI The New Internet?

This self-reflection project I've taken on about a career built with the rise of the internet comes at a very interesting time. Is AI the *next* internet? Time will tell, but the majority seems to believe it will be even bigger—and I agree.

The parallels feel real. In 1998, every company wanted a website but didn't know why. In 2025, every company wants AI but can't articulate the business case. A lot of them *still don't know why*. We're back at the old "gold rush" mentality and FOMO-driven decisions. The difference is that this time the change is happening in months, not years. The internet gave us a decade to adapt, but AI is giving us maybe three years. No technology has ever been adopted as quickly as AI: as of late 2025, AI has accumulated over 1.2 billion users, with faster adoption rates than either smartphones or the internet. If you're not already experimenting, learning, failing fast, and iterating, you're about to get lapped.

If we were blown away by being able to do a simple map and direction lookup on computers in 1998, imagine what might be next? Sitting in your Waymo driverless car while it pulls down directions in real time, finds the best route there, and does this all safer than a human being? And what about all the things we literally can't even imagine AI enabling, because there isn't an earlier precedent for them?

This, my friend, is the dawn of a very new era. We're looking down the barrel of something our grandparents and parents would have never thought possible, or could even fathom. It makes me feel very fortunate to have seen two big breakthroughs like this in my lifetime. There's no telling where this will take us: the only hope is that it's used for good more often than bad, and that it really helps us make advancements and unlock real potential down the road. Medicine, space exploration, fusion: AI might help with all of this, in addition to anything it might do for us in business.

Pittsburgh, The Cradle Of The Next Industrial Revolution?

I can't ignore my physical location when I'm talking about AI and its ancillary offshoots: Pittsburgh. When I moved here over 20 years ago—always easy to remember, as my son was three months old when we did—you could shoot a cannonball down main street and not hit a person, as the saying goes. That was very much the case here. To see where it is now is nothing short of amazing; our county tax collectors are certainly taking full advantage of it by jacking up taxes, let me tell you. After the industrial revolution and the later great steelmaking boom of the sixties and seventies, Pittsburgh was left in an increasingly rough spot as the steel mills closed and that business started to move elsewhere.

Earlier than a lot of other Rust Belt cities, Pittsburgh decided it needed to pivot to a new opportunity. What they chose was colloquially called "Eds and Meds." Having the colleges of University of Pittsburgh and Carnegie Mellon here, the city realized they had two institutions pumping out very smart students (along with the big hospital systems, hence the "meds")—so their challenge simply became how to keep them from moving away. Without going into too much developmental detail, the city has in fact done a great job of doing this, and one could argue it's how we've captured more attention from places like Silicon Valley and elsewhere.

We've reversed the brain-drain to other places, and the statistics show it. Population is up year over year for the first time in a *very* long time; meanwhile, Google, Microsoft, Apple, Meta, and Uber all have a presence here now and are setting up offices, funding research, and so on. That alone can probably stand to illustrate the changes that Pittsburgh is making. Even the fine dining scene is much better: you can hardly even get reservations at places anymore!

Construction is non-stop, more important performing artists are coming to town these days, and they're even shooting more movies here. In general, the city has gone through a great, and seriously important, transformation—and I would argue Cleveland, Buffalo and Detroit are going through the same. Maybe we can call these The Rust Belt Revolutions! Even factories that were closed, or in the process of closing, are now being repurposed to handle the energy needed for the oncoming AI revolution. It gives one hope that, like the days when the country and the world depended on Pittsburgh for their steel, they'll once again depend on it for the energy needed for this next "big thing."

And the story doesn't end there: as of my writing today, on July 15th, 2025, President Trump and Senator David McCormick of Pennsylvania just announced over $90 Billion in investments for energy and AI driven industry, the largest donation ever to the commonwealth of Pennsylvania. Time will tell if that turns into reality.

"For Every CEO That Wants To Talk About ChatGPT, I Will Show You Another 100 That Can't Even Digitally Ship A Product!"

A funny thing happened once I left the MBB firm, which was just as AI was starting to build steam. The MBBs and other consulting firms were getting their go-to-market messaging around it more refined, and were even being deemed "experts" in the practice on it. Experts? Yeah, they were higher up and more well-positioned politically to *call* themselves experts, sure. But realistically, this shit was so new that *nobody* was an expert.

For my part, I noticed that everyone was interested in boarding the AI train, but here we were still regularly dealing with large language model (LLM) issues. There were problems all over the place. What happened to those—did they just go away? I still felt like there was a lot of opportunity to help companies with very basic things, and in fact, I even started posting about it on LinkedIn.

As the subheading above shows, this is what I was experiencing in the market. Everyone wanted to act like they were working in the AI space, but it was still too new for that. Companies had major issues to fix before they even could think about jumping into AI and exploring what it really meant. As an MBB colleague told me in the early days of the consulting firms pushing AI: "Jamie, we have lots of conversations going on with clients about AI, but conversations don't sell."

Three Lessons From My Past That Apply To AI Today

Lesson 1: Start With Personas, Not Technology

Remember when I talked about the large MRO company's transformation and how the California-based design and consulting firm created those detailed personas? "Mike the Maintenance Manager" and all the others plastered on our walls? That framework—starting with *who* will use the technology before deciding *what* technology to use—is exactly what's missing from some AI implementations today.

Companies are rushing to bring in AI solutions for "everyone" without asking: Who specifically needs this? What problem are they trying to solve? A customer service rep needs completely different AI tools than a financial analyst or a warehouse worker. Without personas, you end up with expensive AI tools that sit there unused because they don't actually serve anyone's specific needs.

I'm watching some companies make the same mistake with AI that companies made with their first websites in 1999—building for some generic "users" who don't actually exist. The large MRO company's approach works: identify your key personas first, understand their actual pain points, then design AI solutions that address those specific needs. Otherwise, you're just implementing technology for technology's sake.

Lesson 2: The Three Velocities Problem Still Applies

This relates to the new technology that I helped the Chicago-based QSR get started with, with their core needs summarized by what I described as the *Three Velocities Problem*.

We had *Technology Velocity*, which was how fast our systems could handle new features at a technical level. It was possible to push updates to the app on a hourly basis, but not feasible because of the *Organizational Velocity*, which was how quickly the QSR's vast numbers of employees could learn, adapt, and support these changes. After these two velocities, we had to consider *Market Velocity*—how fast customers in different regions expected or could handle change, because product rollouts in hyper-connected cities would always be handled a little better, and probably more smoothly, than rollouts in places where people weren't as used to rapid change.

Companies trying to implement AI today need to think about these things. They can implement ChatGPT tomorrow (Technology Velocity), but can their people actually use it effectively (Organizational Velocity)? And are their customers ready for AI-powered interactions (Market Velocity)? I'm watching companies push AI at the speed their vendors want to move, not the speed their organizations can absorb. It can lead to some *very* expensive mistakes.

Lesson 3: Never Go Full Big Bang

I'll never forget being called a "dinosaur" at the Bay Area beauty brand for opposing their big bang approach. They ignored my warning, lost millions, and had to roll the whole thing back. That disaster is seared into my memory, and I see companies making the exact same mistake with AI right now.

They want to revolutionize everything at once: AI customer service, AI inventory management, AI financial forecasting, AI everything. All at the same time. To the whole company. What could possibly go wrong?

The gradual, user-group-by-user-group rollout approach we used at the large MRO company—starting with willing early adopters, learning from issues, refining, then expanding—is even more critical with AI. Why? Because AI can fail in ways we don't anticipate, like by hallucinating or otherwise generating completely plausible-sounding nonsense.

You want to catch these issues with a small group of forgiving users, not discover them after you've rolled it out to your entire customer base.

We Need To Up Our Game

Something that's left a lasting impact with me was my experience at the Chicago-based QSR's innovation kitchen in the Chicago suburbs. As part of the French firm work, they would take us out to the innovation kitchen to see how it worked, and to have us actually *make* the QSR's food alongside the real workers. It was really cool, and a great way for us to see inside how our technology was impacting the workers at the front line. I clearly remember standing next to two workers who were showing us how they punched in orders. The woman gave me and my colleagues a skeptical look and asked if the technology we were working on was going to put her and her coworkers out of jobs.

This was around 2017, and back then I could barely fathom that happening—but surprise, surprise—fast forward to 2025 and every Quick Serve Restaurant (QSR) company and other companies are working on figuring exactly this out. Whether it be through kiosks, drive-through ordering, conversational commerce, and so on, organizations are absolutely working to remove fast-food workers from at least some parts of their locations.

And I don't blame them. If you had the opportunity to reduce operating costs, wouldn't you take it? Just like the internet happened to all of us, we took it in stride, upskilled, and made huge leaps to make improvements everywhere. But that said, I'm also a realist, and this technology *does* impact people. What I saw happen at the Chicago-based QSR and elsewhere is that this pivot (AI order-taking at the drive-through, conversational commerce, moves to more kiosks) helped employers focus on more highly-strategic and value-based activities—and more on their employees, too. So now, instead of several employees sitting behind the counter only taking orders, a very basic and repetitive task, you can pull them out of there and focus them on more high-value things like cleaner restaurants, more considerate customer service, and guaranteeing a greater customer journey overall that equates to both happier customers *and* employees.

Still, though others may disagree, I believe that the gains we make as a society with technology far outweigh the job losses that come with it. This may change over time; I just haven't seen it happen yet. The key saying we've all heard on this subject is that AI won't replace your jobs—it will be the people that *use AI better than you* that will replace your jobs. However, seeing the headlines lately, I think lots of people would disagree.

At last check, McKinsey says that up to 14% of the workforce will need to "re-position" their jobs by 2030 based on this technological upheaval. I listen to a podcast (the Every Day AI Podcast, thanks Mark for turning me on to that!) where the host, Jordan Wilson, has a salient point. People shouldn't be thinking about "upskilling" for AI, and they need to "un-learn" what they have learned in the past. This will help them to adapt to AI more quickly. I tend to agree that, while the patterns, frameworks and hype cycles are similar to others we have seen in the past, the technology isn't, and this does truly seem to be game-changing tech that is coming at a rapid pace. I'm not going to tell you to fasten your seatbelts or "buckle up," but to paraphrase Bob Dylan, we'd better start swimming or we'll sink like stones.

What Will This Mean For The Next Generation?

I often think about the impact on kids who are either in college or just coming out of it. They aren't looking at the same opportunities, or even reality—especially financially—that I faced at that age. I think there'll be a blend of practical skills needed (or to go to the extreme end, Nvidia CEO Jensen Huang recently projected that the most highly-skilled labor needed would be in plumbing, electrical and carpeting), but those who use them in combination with technology will absolutely have a leg up. I tell kids who want to go into any field to try to learn and master AI with it, as I'm sure every other mentor is doing, and I'm sure all kids are realizing. That way they can provide more value for the older colleagues that don't have it mastered (or don't want to.)

And that's great, but only as long as it doesn't come at the cost of not doing things like having conversations, connecting with people *offline*, or having your own critical thinking to add value.

On the flip side, what does it mean for our generation? I think those of us who went through the early internet phase and are Gen X or adjacent are best-positioned to both embrace this next AI revolution and realize we must blend humanity into it to really make the gains and traction we need as a society. As I sit here, aged 50, I realize it's been a wild ride from the nineties to here: I've surely had a lot of ups and downs, but I wouldn't trade it for anything. And it's amazing that we're about to embark on another wild ride: this time with the knowledge and wisdom to really position ourselves better for it (I am an optimist). More importantly, we also have the opportunity to use those superpowers, experiences, and stories to *help* others as they go through it themselves, and hopefully make their experiences even richer as they embark on this journey. We can even learn from them!

🔑 Chapter Takeaways: The Next "Internet"?

1. We've Seen This Movie Before, But It's Bigger Now
   Just like the internet transformed everything, generative AI is doing it again at warp speed. If you've already lived through one tech upheaval, you're better-prepared to ride the next

wave. Just try to stay aware, adaptable, and humble in the face
of things you might not always understand.

2. Location Still Matters—Especially In The Rust Belt Rebirth
   Pittsburgh is a city that's pivoting from steel to software, and
   is now positioning itself to be a heart of AI's energy and innovation surge. It's a reminder that reinvention is possible, both
   geographically and personally.

3. Buzz Does Not Equal Breakthrough
   Everyone wants to talk about AI, but few can implement it
   meaningfully. Behind the scenes, many companies still can't
   even digitize basic operations. The noise is high, and the need
   for grounded, pragmatic advisors is higher.

4. The Innovation Vs. Impact Dilemma
   That question in the Chicago-based QSR's innovation kitch-
   en—"Is this tech going to replace us?"—sticks in my head.
   The gains of AI are real, but so are the human costs. The future
   will probably belong to those who lead with efficiency as well
   as empathy.

5. Skills Will Change, But Character Still Wins
   Yes, the next generation needs to master AI. But soft skills like
   real conversation, empathy, and critical thinking, will become
   rarer and more meaningful. The winners will have tech flu-
   ency, but also tech-plus-humanity.

6. Gen X Can Be The Bridge
   My generation—raised analog, trained digital—is perfectly-posi-
   tioned to lead. Not by knowing it all, but by combining wisdom,
   curiosity, and the experience to guide others through noise.

7. The Best Use Of This Moment Is Service

I've been shaped by disruptions before, but this time, I'm not just surviving and thriving—I'm here to serve. The highest leverage I have now is sharing what I've learned to help others navigate, adapt, and rise to the top of the new market.

CHAPTER 11

How Recognizing The Same Patterns Might Save You Time And Money

After twenty-five-plus years in tech, through Y2K hysteria, dot-com crashes, social media revolutions, and now AI madness, I've developed what you might call pattern recognition. It's not that I'm smarter than anyone else—I've just seen this movie enough times to know when the plot's about to twist.

Every CEO I meet wants to talk about AI. Fair enough. But when they lean forward and ask, "How do we implement this without disrupting everything?"—well, that's when I know my particular brand of been-there-done-that actually means something. Because I asked that same question about e-commerce in 2010, about mobile apps in 2015, and about cloud migration in 2018. The technology changes, but the fear is eternal.

Why Experience Across Multiple Tech Waves Matters

The Déjà Vu Factor

What nobody tells you about technology revolutions is that they're remarkably predictable. I'm not talking about which specific technology wins—nobody saw TikTok coming—but the human reactions and the corporate responses follow a script so consistent you could set your watch to it.

I was at a board meeting last month where an executive asked his team, "What's our AI strategy?" The room went quiet, and then everyone started talking at once about ChatGPT, machine learning, automation. I'd heard this exact conversation before, just with different buzzwords. In 2001 it was "What's our internet strategy?" In 2008 it was "What's our social media strategy?" In 2016 it was "What's our cloud strategy?"

The pattern never changes: existential corporate fear, followed by frantic activity, followed by massive spending, followed by eventual rationalization. If you've lived through multiple cycles, you can help companies skip straight to rationalization and save themselves millions.

Translating Between Eras

The real value of multi-wave experience isn't just recognizing patterns—it's being able to translate between them. When a retail CEO tells me they're worried about AI disrupting their business model, I don't start with tools and neural networks. I start with, "Remember when everyone thought Amazon would kill you in 2010? You survived that. Let me show you why this is actually the same problem with different packaging."

This translation ability is important because most executives don't have time to become technology experts. They need someone who can explain that implementing AI is less like learning a new language and more like adding another channel to their omnichannel strategy—something they've already done successfully.

I was sitting with the CMO of a major retailer who was panicking about generative AI creating infinite personalized content. "Our competitors will bury us," he said. I pulled up my laptop and showed him a presentation from 2012 about programmatic advertising—another technology that was supposed to make human marketers obsolete.

"Look," I told him, "same promises, same vendors even, just different underlying tech. You adapted to that, you'll adapt to this."

Knowing What Actually Sticks

Want to know a secret? Of every hundred "revolutionary" technologies I've seen launched with great fanfare, maybe ten become permanent parts of the business landscape. The rest either die quietly or get absorbed into something else.

Remember when every company needed a Second Life presence? When QR codes were going to change everything? When blockchain was going to eliminate intermediaries? I sat through a lot of presentations on any of these and more, and spent real money helping companies implement some of them. Most are footnotes now.

But eCommerce? That stuck. Mobile apps? Stuck. Cloud computing? Definitely stuck. The pattern is always the same: the technologies that survive are the ones that solve real problems for real people in ways that are meaningfully better than what came before. Everything else is just expensive noise or add ons or features to that core tech.

This is why it's important that I've gone through multiple waves of tech. When you've seen enough technologies fail, you develop a sixth sense for which ones have staying power. AI? That's staying. The metaverse? Check back in five years, but I have my doubts. Quantum computing for everyday business use? I'll believe it when I see it.

The Relationship Capital Compound Effect

What they don't teach in business school is that the people you meet in tech wave one become the leaders of tech wave three. That principal engineer struggling with JavaScript in 2003? She's now the CTO making decisions about AI implementation. The hungry sales rep who cold-called me about cloud storage in 2012? He's running part-nerships at a major AI company now.

My phone contains more than twenty-five years of these relation-ships. Need to understand loyalty at scale? I worked on the app for a huge multinational QSR that now drives 40% of their revenue. Stuck on a B2B eCommerce challenge? I was there when a very important MRO company figured it out the first time. I'm not trying to name-drop; this is the compound interest of staying in the game long enough to watch everyone grow up.

Last week, a client needed to understand how AI might impact their supply chain. Instead of commissioning a study, I organized a call with three people: someone who digitized supply chains in 2008, someone who mobilized them in 2015, and someone who's currently implementing AI in logistics. Three hours, probably $500 in steaks and wine, and my client got insights that would have cost $500,000 from a consulting firm.

Scar Tissue as Strategy

Every consultant has war stories. The difference is whether you learned from them. I've got enough scar tissue from failed imple-mentations to know exactly what kills technology transformations, and spoiler alert: it's rarely the technology.

Remember my story about the Bay Area beauty brand? The one where they called me a dinosaur for opposing their big bang approach? That disaster cost them millions, but it taught me something valuable: the most dangerous person in any transformation is the executive who's read just enough to be confident but not enough to be com-petent. I see the same thing with AI now—executives who've done a weekend course on ChatGPT suddenly thinking they're ready to reshape their entire organization. It's those people or executives who take a curious approach to the situation or technology, are open to other people's ideas, and who believe in a fail-fast-and-change model that are typically successful.

The scar tissue teaches you to spot the warning signs. When I hear "We'll figure out the data governance later" or "Our people will adapt" or my personal favorite, "This time it's different," I know exactly where we're headed. The great thing is that I can now short-circuit these disasters before they happen. I've seen every variation of failure at least twice.

The Advantage of Recognizing Patterns In Tech Development

The Three-Phase Pattern

Every technology follows the same lifecycle: Experimentation, Standardization, Commoditization. Always. Without exception. Understanding where we are in that cycle determines everything about how you should approach it.

Experimentation is the Wild West. Think internet in 1996, mobile apps in 2008, AI in 2022. Everything's expensive, nothing's standardized, and half the vendors will be dead in two years. This is when you should be learning, not betting the farm.

Standardization is when patterns emerge. E-commerce platforms in 2010, cloud services in 2015, AI right now in 2025. The winners are becoming clear, best practices are emerging, and costs are dropping fast. This is when you should be implementing.

Commoditization is when it's just another tool. Email, basic websites, standard mobile apps—hell, you could even say eCommerce in some cases now. The competitive advantage is gone, but so is most of the risk. This is when you should be optimizing.

The expensive mistake is getting these phases wrong. Betting big during Experimentation (unless you're enormously well-funded), waiting until Commoditization to start (you're now officially behind), or treating Standardization like it's still Experimentation (paralysis by analysis).

The Recurring Cast of Characters

In every tech wave, the same characters appear. There's the Visionary CEO who goes all-in too early and either becomes a case study or a cautionary tale. The Fast Follower who waits for someone else to take the damage then executes flawlessly. The Skeptical CFO who needs ROI projections for technologies that don't have precedents yet. The Eager Vendor who promises everything and delivers half.

Knowing these archetypes helps you navigate the human side of transformation. When I meet with a leadership team, I can usually identify each character within the first hour. More importantly, I know what each one needs to hear to get on board. The Visionary needs to feel like a pioneer. The CFO needs risk mitigation. The Fast Follower needs competitive benchmarks.

The Human Problems Never Change

Here's the thing that would be funny if it weren't so expensive: with all our technological advancement, the things that derail implementations haven't changed since I started in this business. It's still politics, fear, and incompetence—just with fancier PowerPoints.

Middle managers still sabotage changes that threaten their fiefdoms. Executives still want revolutionary results without revolutionary changes. IT departments still say no to everything new while simultaneously complaining about being seen as roadblocks. The technology gets exponentially more sophisticated, but we're still the same messy humans trying to work together.

This is actually good news if you've seen it before. When a client tells me their AI initiative is stalling, I don't start with the technology.

I start with, "Who's threatened by this?" Nine times out of ten, that question leads directly to the real problem.

Speed Is The Only Real Difference

The patterns are identical, but the tempo is accelerating. The internet had a decade-long adoption curve. Mobile was five years. AI? We're looking at three years, max, between "what's that?" and "table stakes."

This acceleration makes pattern recognition even more valuable. When you have less time to make decisions, you need experience. You can't afford to learn everything from scratch when the entire landscape changes every six months.

I tell clients who are excited by AI demos that the vendors selling you this technology have never run your business, or felt the pain of a failed digital implementation, or had to explain to a board why millions got burned on the "next big thing." I have, though. The thing about being in this industry so long is that you start to see which promises are real and which are just expensive illusions—or hallucinations, more appropriate for AI—in a new package.

What This Means For You

I'm not saying experience is everything. There are brilliant 25-year-olds out there building the future while I'm still trying to figure out why my printer won't connect to my WiFi. But if you're a company trying to navigate technological change without destroying what already works, you need someone who's seen enough cycles to know the difference between evolution and revolution.

That's what pattern recognition gives you: the ability to move fast without breaking everything. To know which consultants are selling snake oil and which ones actually know their stuff. To spot the difference between a technology that will transform your industry and one that will drain your budget and disappear.

Every company I work with now gets the benefit of every mistake I've seen, every success I've witnessed, every pattern I've recognized. When they ask about AI, they're not just getting AI advice—they're getting it filtered through two decades of watching technologies succeed and fail.

The future isn't about the technology. It never has been. It's about understanding how humans adapt to change, how organizations evolve, and how markets respond to innovation. Those patterns are as reliable as gravity.

So when someone asks me what makes me different from all the other consultants pitching AI transformation, I tell them straight: I've been transformed before. Multiple times. And I'm still here.

That's the pattern advantage. Not predicting the future, but recognizing it when it starts to rhyme with the past.

The Parallel Change Playbook

Before you put this book down, I want to leave you with one last tool—a way to think about change, whether it be AI, digital disruption, or the next big wave that we haven't even named yet.

I call it the **Parallel Change Playbook.** It's built on the simple truth that technologies change, but human adaptation follows the same arc every time. If you understand the pattern, you can shorten the pain, accelerate trust, and lead others through uncertainty.

Step 1: Identify the Fear

Every shift begins with anxiety. People wonder: Will I lose my job? My value? Even my *identity*? You can't solve change if you don't name the fear.

Step 2: Translate to Enablement

Reframe the new tool as something that *amplifies* what you're doing instead of replaces you. Show how it frees them from drudgery and gives them leverage.

Step 3: Prototype in Safe Zones

Run small, low-stakes pilots. Let people see proof of value in their own work before scaling.

Step 4: Institutionalize What Works

Bake the wins into training, process, and culture. Make adoption the default, not the exception.

This pattern has held true from eCommerce, to cloud, to remote work, and to AI. The technologies may look new, but the playbook is not.

So as you step into your next chapter, don't just ride the wave. Lead it. With clarity, courage, and a playbook in hand, you're more ready than you think.

Bonus Material: The E2I Framework

E2I: From Experience to Intelligence

Before the book ends, I'd like to share something I've been cooking for a while. It's just a teaser, but please stay tuned for more like this in 2026!

Though you've reached the end of this book, the real work is just beginning. We've explored my personal journey of career navigation and reinvention, and I'm proud of my resilience, but I want to say that to succeed sustainably in the modern era also requires a framework. I've distilled this into what I call the E2I shift: moving from Experience to Intelligence.

The rules of any career have pretty much always been the same: accumulate experience. That's been about it. We treat our past, from the years and our various roles, to our scars and our successes, as a raw, unstructured stockpile of memories, and these give us the muscle memory and instinct to navigate new challenges that appear to us. But in an economy defined by rapid change and automation, raw experience isn't quite as useful as it used to be. Now, it's more like an illustration of our potential.

But don't worry: you can still do something with that. I want to challenge you with the E2I framework to take your life's raw material and process it into something like a set of rules. It's about transforming your unstructured "past" into structured intelligence, which becomes a kind of repeatable, scalable operating system of your own making.

E2I TRANSFORMATION

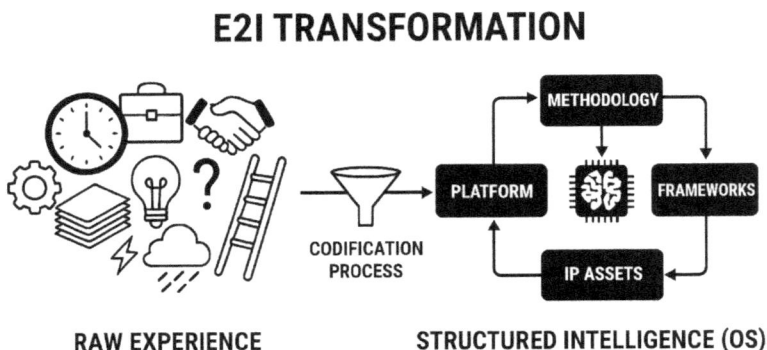

RAW EXPERIENCE   CODIFICATION PROCESS   **STRUCTURED INTELLIGENCE (OS)**

The difference here is between being a "knowledge worker" who rents out their time to solve problems one by one and an **asset-owner** who has built a set of methods they can follow for themselves. When you set your wisdom into stone using frameworks you've built, processes, and intellectual property, you stop reinventing the wheel in front of new challenges every Monday morning, and you start building a machine that drives your future.

The opportunity in front of you now is not just to find your next job, but to define your own platform. Whether you deploy the intelligence that makes you You to drive innovation within a major organization or to carve out an independent path, the principle I'm trying to convey here is that **_you're_ no longer just the holder of a job title, beholden to someone else's roadmap. You are the architect and owner of your own intellectual capital.**

The page has turned: the question isn't just *"What's Next for Me?"* anymore, but *"How will I structure what I know into assets that I own?"* The tools, the maps, and the strategies to operationalize this shift are waiting. So get going, and build your own intelligence system!

CONCLUSION

Your Next Bold Move Is Waiting

If you've made it this far, thank you. Not just for reading, but for showing up—for yourself.

I wrote this book to equip you, more than anything else. I definitely wasn't trying to impress you.

You've walked with me through the highs of strategy rooms and startup bets, the lows of burnout, layoffs, and gut-wrenching pivots, and the raw middle where most of us live: uncertain, in motion, and rewriting our scripts in real-time. You've seen how I stumbled through the early digital era, how I rebuilt after corporate bruises, and how I leveraged my experience to carve out something that actually felt like mine. And how I'm still doing it now, in the middle of another major shift, with AI and automation changing the rules yet again.

But more than my story, I wanted this book to be a kind of mirror for you.

Your circumstances are different from mine, but your goals are the same: to reclaim clarity in your life, to redefine success on your terms, to lead with curiosity and openness about the future instead of fear, and finally, to *use your damn voice.*

Whether you're climbing a corporate ladder, building a one-person empire, or somewhere in between, your next chapter is about honoring your truth, and aligning your work with who you actually are.

With my book, you now hopefully have the stories, tools, and patterns. But of course, the change will come from the decisions you might make after you put this book down.

I'd like to suggest a pause here. Let's think about where you've been, and then ask—what's my next bold move?

Maybe it's a conversation, or a shift in how you lead; maybe it's finally making the leap into something you've been thinking about for a long time.

Whatever it is, I hope you won't wait.

Your past has prepared you, and the world is shifting fast. Your signal is needed now, more than ever.

Time to go build. Let's get to it.

Acknowledgements

I never would have written this book without the help and support of the many people and experiences that all led up to it, but most important was the foundation my parents, Jim and Janet, gave me. They taught me to always be hard-working, but gave me the freedom and opportunities to also put me in a place to craft my own path, question things, and always be curious. I also benefited hugely from the support of my sister Bridget and my aunts and uncles growing up: your love and support helped give me the comfort and confidence to tackle "this thing we call life."

To Catherine, Kyle, and Nora: thank you for cheering me on, for your patience, for your understanding, and for giving me the space to allow me to pursue this endeavor. Thank you also for NOT laughing me out of the room when I first floated this idea years ago. You are my grounding force.

To Teresa Mueller, thank you not only for being a fantastic mother for our children but also for being supportive when I did crazy things like wanting to quit a job with no plan or becoming an independent consultant.

This book also wouldn't exist without the people who helped me navigate the messy middle of reinvention. I'd like to thank the mentors, colleagues, friends, and family (my extended, Oligeri and Renillo families) who showed up at exactly the right time, in exactly the right way, as well as:

Matt Doan for taking a chance on me to help mentor, coach, and shape how I approached the "new normal." My Corporate Graduation colleagues who helped encourage and push me along on this journey, and specifically Matt and David Tarr for helping with suggestions and edits.

The countless people who helped me get this book published: Barry Adler for encouraging me to first write the outline and plugging me in with his writing network, Robert Morgan for coming on board to help edit this mess, Patrick Coletti and Whitney Gossett who then led me to my publisher, Maria Ramirez. Mukul Pandya (again) for the support, guidance and additional editing steers. Joe Davis and Peter Millerd for the calls and messages giving me advice on how best to approach the publishing, marketing and advertising of the book.

My earliest teachers and colleagues from Blessed Sacrament grade school (where I first learned to code on a Macintosh!), Cathedral Prep High School, the University of Dayton, The University of Pennsylvania, and The Wharton School—thank you for sparking my curiosity about technology, people, and possibility. You helped me see that every "what the hell is this?" moment is really an invitation to grow.

All my classmates and teachers in the schools mentioned above for the encouragement and support they gave me. My University of Dayton water polo coaches Sean Geehan, Francis Martinez, Bill Whiting (and plenty others!), and teammates for showing me what hard work, team work and dedication can get you. They helped refine my work ethic, skills and goal-setting capabilities.

My mentors and advocates during my time at Wharton for believing in me and encouraging me to advance my career and experiences; Mukul Pandya, Lynn Phillips, Bruce Brownstein, Bill Dunworth, Jason Wingard and countless others. All the mentors, leaders, colleagues, family and friends that helped me on this journey, whether that be listening, feedback or encouragement; Steve Hay, Bob Barr, Kris Rhen, Chad Sitler, Amy Shields, Dave Rebman, Anjum Merchant, Jeff Werness, Mike Razzoog, Mike Casulla, Simon Lew, Adam Zoghlin, EJ Onweller, Dee Burger, Dwayne Doshier, Mark Neihaus, Balaji Venkatesan, Lina Murton, Jenn Carlson, Jenna

Dingman, Steve Beir, Peter Maloof, Rob Holland, Jason Hatch, Alex Christen, Ted Levine, Matt Cava, Dan Coyne, Jay Venkat, Simone Woodhouse, Mike Troisi, Samer Najia, Ian Leibovici, Harsh Jain, Kevin Solchenberger, Kelly O'Connor, Paras Malik, Kaison Morris, Lance Cibik, Cecilia Doan, Michael Gardon, Todd Inskeep, Brian Smith, Nathaniel Yap, Scott Cannizaro, Mark Kilgore, Mark Arbogast, Wendy Rosploch, Kate Beardsley, Jon Nordmark, and all the countless others (please accept my apologies if you're left out, but again, to so many of you, thank you!)

To the leaders, teams, clients, and collaborators I've had the privilege to learn from across consulting, digital transformation, and AI, thank you for trusting me to help you make sense of change. Your courage to experiment shaped much of what's written here.

And to the reader, thank you for being here. By picking up this book, you're part of the conversation I first saw years ago: how to stay human, curious, and clear-headed in the middle of industry-wide disruption. That's what this journey has always been about.

To those of you walking your own version of "what's next": this one's for you.